SWEET AND SAVORY SWEDISH BAKING

LEILA LINDHOLM

# Sweet and Savory Swedish Baking

Skyhorse Publishing

# my kitchen heroes

I've loved baking for as long as I can remember. My Mum never missed an opportunity to tie aprons around us ready for a big baking session, and my Granny was a keen baker too. I can remember standing on a stool in my grandmother's kitchen as a three-year old, putting a sticky mixture into muffin cases. The best bit was licking the bowl clean afterwards—I never missed out on that!

The best recipes are passed down, from one generation to the next being adapted, polished, and preserved like family treasures. That is part of the magic of baking. I am not the kind of person to keep recipes secret. Why do that when you can give those around you—and yourself—so many happy moments with delicious cakes, breads, and buns?

When I was young, I was an honorary member of a baking club called the Muffin Mafia. It consisted of me, a neighbor, Aunt Elsa, and a crew of other aunts. I'm not quite sure how many other members there were besides myself and Aunt Elsa—I suspect that my aunt started the club mainly for my benefit and, boy, did I think it was exciting! The purpose of the club was to exchange recipes via letters (an early form of communication), which were then tested and entered into a charming little notebook. I used to rush to Elsa's at every opportunity, and there I learned to bake delicious muffins, bread, buns, and sponges.

I thought the whole thing was fantastic, and looking back I realize how clever Elsa was to conjure up a sense of mystique around baking and recipes. For a small child (and probably for many adults, too), it's almost magical to see beautiful and tasty cakes and breads arising from little more than a few eggs, a bag of flour, and some sugar.

Baking with your kids or grandchildren is a superb pastime. There's something special about sharing the magic of creation. It works no matter how old or young you are, and for me it has been a lifelong romance with masses of happy memories together with friends and relatives. I hope to share some of this with you, too. Some people say life is a bowl of cherries, but for me it's a plate of freshly baked buns and a glass of berry squash!

Bake with love, Leila

# in the cookie jar

It's not always easy to keep your hands out of the cookie jar. Those cookies look so terribly tempting standing there in the pantry, and just knowing how they taste is enough to make your mouth water. Fortunately, many cookies are at their best when freshly baked, so the problem tends to solve itself through regular coffee mornings. Biscotti, on the other hand, ought to sit on that shelf a little bit longer . . .

# four different chocolate chip cookies

This is my favorite chocolate chip cookie recipe. You can make the cookie dough in advance and keep it in the freezer for a few weeks. Then all you have to do is take the dough out of the freezer, slice, and bake! You can vary the recipe with all kinds of delicious flavors.

MAKES 25 COOKIES
BASIC RECIPE
½ cup unsalted butter, softened
½ cup demerara sugar
1 organic egg
¾ cup all-purpose flour
¼ cup rolled oats
½ tablespoon baking powder
¼ tablespoon salt
4 oz good quality dark chocolate (70% cocoa solids)
zest of 1 lime

1. Beat the butter and the sugar until creamy. Mix in the egg.
2. Mix the flour, rolled oats, baking powder, and salt and blend into the dough.
3. Chop the chocolate coarsely and mix into the dough together with the lime zest.
4. Shape the dough into a roll 2 in thick and roll it up in parchment paper or plastic wrap. Put the dough in the freezer for about 30 minutes.
5. Preheat the oven to 350°F.
6. Cut the roll into half-inch thick slices and put them on a baking sheet lined with parchment paper.
7. Bake the cookies in the center of the oven for about 10 minutes or until golden.

## white chocolate chip ginger cookies

MAKES 25 COOKIES
1 batch of cookie dough, see basic recipe
4 oz good-quality white chocolate (instead of dark chocolate)
1 ½ in fresh root ginger

1. Prepare the cookie dough according to the basic recipe, but replace the dark chocolate with white chocolate and add the peeled and grated ginger when you mix the butter and sugar.

## chocolate chip orange cookies

MAKES 25 COOKIES
1 batch of cookie dough, see basic recipe
¼ cup unsweetened coconut (instead of rolled oats)
zest of 2 oranges (instead of 1 lime)

1. Prepare the cookie dough according to the basic recipe, but replace the rolled oats with unsweetened coconut and replace the lime zest with orange zest.

## chocolate chip peanut cookies

MAKES 25 COOKIES
1 batch of cookie dough, see basic recipe
½ cup salted peanuts

1. Prepare the cookie dough according to the basic recipe and add chopped peanuts with the other dry ingredients.

# sugar & spice

Sugar comes from sugar cane and sugar beet and has different characteristics depending on how it has been prepared.

## Muscovado sugar

Muscovado is a wickedly rich-tasting sugar that is traditionally made from the sugar cane grown in Mauritius. In contrast to white granular sugar, muscovado sugar is raw, unrefined sugar, and it has a natural color and distinctive flavor. It's taste is similar to demerara sugar but richer. The dark variety has a definite licorice accent, while the light variety has a caramel flavor. Muscovado sugar is used in desserts, and it works very well with chocolate. It can also be used to make ice cream and in baking bread and cookies. My mum loves using it in Irish coffee. Delicious!

## Confectioner's sugar

Confectioner's sugar is finely ground granular sugar with some added anti-caking agent to prevent clumping. It is used when you want to sweeten something without the sugar crystals being visible or felt. It is used in icing, toppings, or to sweeten cream or yogurt. You can also dust it over cakes or desserts for a finishing touch.

## Caster sugar

Caster sugar is the most widely used for cakes and pastries. It is made by purifying and refining sugar beet or sugar cane, giving it a pure white color. Superfine caster sugar is ideal for baking, but regular granulated sugar is acceptable.

## Demerara sugar (also known as turbinado sugar)

Demerara sugar consists of sugar crystals made from dark brown sugar cane syrup, which gives it a special piquant accent in contrast to the neutral sweetness of white granular sugar. You can use it for sweetening in bakery and desserts and also to liven up sauces, marinades, and casseroles.

## Vanilla sugar

Vanilla adds a special touch to many cakes and cookies. There are different kinds of vanilla sugar and the type I've used in many of my recipes has the consistency of confectioner's sugar. If you can't get hold of it in your local shop, it's easy to make your own. Just add a split vanilla pod or two to an airtight container containing about 1 cup of confectioner's sugar and leave to stand for a couple of weeks. Alternatively, use a couple of dried up vanilla pods and mix them with about 2 cups of granulated sugar in a blender until you get a powdery consistency. Soon you won't be able to bake without it, and you'll never go back to using synthetic vanilla essence again.

# coconut pyramids

This recipe is absolutely wonderful and you just have to try it out. The trick is to mix lime zest in the mixture. I usually dip the base of the coconut pyramids in melted chocolate and leave them to set in paper cases or on a wire rack. Coconut and chocolate are an irresistible combination of flavors!

MAKES 16 PYRAMIDS

1/4 cup unsalted butter

2 organic eggs

1/2 cup sugar

3 1/4 cups unsweetened coconut

zest of 1 lime

1 tablespoon Amaretto liquor or rum

1. Preheat the oven to 350°F.
2. Melt the butter and mix it with the other ingredients.
3. Let the mixture rise for about 10 minutes.
4. Shape the mixture into pyramids on a baking sheet lined with parchment paper.
5. Bake in the center of the oven for about 15 minutes or until golden.

# french madeleines

These small, shell-shaped and incredibly tasty French cakes are almost as soft as mini sponges. You will need Madeleine tins or some other kind of small cupcake pans.

MAKES 12 MADELEINES

1/4 cup plus 2 tablespoons butter, softened

1/4 cup plus 2 tablespoons granulated sugar

1 teaspoon vanilla sugar

zest of 1 lemon

2 organic eggs

3/4 cup plus 2 tablespoons all-purpose flour

1 teaspoon baking powder

butter and dried breadcrumbs for the madeleine or small cupcake pans

1. Preheat the oven to 350°F.
2. Beat together the butter, sugar, vanilla sugar, and lime zest until light and creamy.
3. Mix in the eggs.
4. Mix together the flour and baking powder and blend into the mixture.
5. Grease and coat the cake pans with breadcrumbs.
6. Spoon the mixture into the pans and bake in the center of the oven for 10 minutes or until golden.

# saffron biscotti

**MAKES 35 PIECES**

½ cup unsalted butter
1 pinch of saffron
2 organic eggs
⅔ cup sugar
3 cups all-purpose flour
1 ½ teaspoons baking powder
½ cup almonds

1. Preheat the oven to 350°F.
2. Melt the butter and mix in the saffron. Pour in the butter into a bowl and beat in the eggs.
3. Mix the dry ingredients with the whole almonds and blend into the saffron butter.
4. Shape the dough into three loaves and put them on a baking sheet lined with parchment paper.
5. Bake in the center of the oven for about 25 minutes.
6. Take out the loaves and reduce the temperature to 250°F.
7. Cut the loaves into half-inch slices. Return the slices to the baking sheet.
8. Leave to dry in the center of the oven for about 15 minutes.

# biscotti di prato

These yummy, crunchy treats originate from Tuscany, where they are often served together with the Italian dessert wine, Vin Santo. The biscotti is dipped in the sweet wine just as we dunk our cookies in coffee.

MAKES 30 PIECES

1/2 cup almonds
3/4 cup pine nuts
1/2 vanilla pod
2 1/3 cups all-purpose flour
3/4 cup sugar
zest of 1 orange
1/4 teaspoon baking powder
1 pinch of salt
2 organic eggs

1. Preheat the oven to 350°F.
2. Blanch the almonds. Toast them in the oven for about 5 minutes until they turn lightly brown.
3. Chop the almonds and the pine nuts coarsely. Split the vanilla pod lengthways and scrape out the seeds.
4. Mix together the chopped almonds and pine nuts, the vanilla seeds, flour, sugar, orange zest, baking powder, and salt on a clean surface.
5. Make a well in the center and crack in the eggs.
6. Work everything into a dough and shape it into two long rolls.
7. Bake on a baking sheet lined with parchment paper in the center of the oven for about 25 minutes. Cut through one of the rolls to make sure they are completely done.
8. Reduce the temperature to 250°F.
9. Cut the rolls at an angle into half-inch slices. Return the slices to the baking sheet.
10. Leave to dry in the center of the oven for about 25 minutes or until completely dry.

# chocolate biscotti with olives

I came up with the idea for this recipe while I was wondering whether chocolate and olives would mix. Adding pine nuts gave the biscotti a brilliant extra tweak!

MAKES 25 PIECES

1 organic egg

2/3 cup sugar

2 cups all-purpose flour

3 1/2 tablespoons good quality cocoa powder

1 teaspoon baking powder

1/2 teaspoon salt

1/2 cup pitted black olives

1/2 cup pine nuts

4 oz good-quality dark chocolate (70% cocoa solids)

1/4 cup olive oil

3 tablespoons cold water

1. Preheat the oven to 300°F.
2. Beat together the egg and the sugar until pale and fluffy.
3. Mix together the flour, cocoa powder, baking powder, and salt and blend into the egg mixture.
4. Chop the olives, pine nuts, and chocolate coarsely and stir into the egg mixture.
5. Add the olive oil and water and work into a sticky dough.
6. Shape the dough into long rolls and put them on a baking sheet lined with parchment paper.
7. Bake in the center of the oven for about 25 minutes. Take the rolls out and reduce the temperature to 250°F.
8. Cut the rolls into half-inch slices. Return the slices to the baking sheet and leave to dry in the center of the oven for about 20 minutes.

# cardamom biscotti

MAKES 35 PIECES

1 teaspoon cardamom pods

1 vanilla pod

1/2 cup unsalted butter, softened

1/2 cup sugar

1/4 cup demerara sugar

2 organic eggs

1/3 cup almonds

1 dried bitter almond

3 cups all-purpose flour

1 1/2 teaspoons baking powder

1. Preheat the oven to 350°F.
2. Pound the cardamom pods in a mortar. Split the vanilla pod lengthways and scrape out the seeds.
3. Beat together the butter, sugar, demerara sugar, vanilla seeds, and cardamom until creamy.
4. Stir in one egg at a time.
5. Chop the almonds coarsely and grate the bitter almond.
6. Mix the almonds and the bitter almond with the flour and baking powder. Fold into the mixture.
7. Shape the dough into two long rolls and put them on a baking sheet lined with parchment paper.
8. Bake in the center of the oven for about 25 minutes. Take the rolls out and reduce the temperature to 250°F.
9. Cut the rolls into half-inch slices and return the slices to the oven.
10. Leave to dry in the center of the oven for about 10 minutes or until completely dry.

# almond butter cookies

We served these classic cookies at one of my first jobs. They are really simple to make and are perfect both for a coffee break and as an accompaniment to a dessert. We used to serve them together with rhubarb soup and crème brûlée.

MAKES 60 COOKIES

3/4 cup plus 2 tablespoons unsalted
    butter, softened
1 cup sugar
zest of 1 lemon
2 cups all-purpose flour
3 organic eggs
1 cup slivered almonds

1. Preheat the oven to 350°F.
2. Beat the butter, the sugar, and the lemon zest until creamy.
3. Carefully fold the flour into the mixture and finally stir in one egg at a time.
4. Pipe the mixture into 3–4 in long strings on a baking sheet lined with parchment paper. Space them well apart.
5. Decorate the mixture with slivered almonds and bake in the center of the oven for 4–6 minutes or until golden.

# grandma's brittle cookies

My grandmother absolutely loves cookies with her coffee. This is a very good, basic recipe that can be used for several different kinds of cookie.

MAKES 50 COOKIES
BASIC RECIPE

3/4 cup plus 2 tablespoons unsalted
    butter, softened
1 teaspoon vanilla sugar
1/3 cup sugar
2 3/4–3 cups all-purpose flour

1. Preheat the oven to 350°F.
2. Beat together the butter, the vanilla sugar, and the sugar until pale and fluffy.
3. Add the flour and work into a dough, but don't knead.
4. Put the dough in a plastic bag and leave to rest in the refrigerator for at least 1 hour.
5. Pick a flavoring of your choice (see the variations on page 22).

# chocolate & hazelnut cookies

MAKES 50 COOKIES

1 batch of cookie dough, see basic
    recipe page 21
4 oz good-quality dark chocolate (70%
    cocoa solids)
1 cup hazelnuts

1. Prepare the cookie dough according to the basic recipe.
2. Preheat the oven to 350°F.
3. Chop the chocolate and the hazelnuts coarsely and knead
   them into the dough, reserving some hazelnuts for decoration.
4. Roll the dough into small balls and flatten them on a baking
   sheet lined with parchment paper. Put one hazelnut on each
   cookie.
5. Bake in the center of the oven for about 10 minutes or until
   lightly golden.

# orange & pine nut cookies

MAKES 50 COOKIES

1 batch of cookie dough, see basic
    recipe page 21
zest of 2 oranges
3/4 cup pine nuts

1. Prepare the cookie dough according to the basic recipe.
2. Preheat the oven to 350°F.
3. Knead the orange zest and the pine nuts into the dough,
   reserving some pine nuts for decoration.
4. Roll the dough into small balls and flatten them on a baking
   sheet lined with parchment paper. Put one pine nut on each
   cookie.
5. Bake in the center of the oven for about 10 minutes or until
   lightly golden.

# raspberry cookies

MAKES 50 COOKIES

1 batch of cookie dough, see basic
    recipe page 21
1/3 cup raspberry jam

1. Prepare the cookie dough according to the basic recipe.
2. Preheat the oven to 350°F.
3. Roll the dough into small balls and flatten them on a baking
   sheet lined with parchment paper.
4. Use your finger to make a small well in the center of each
   cookie. Place a small amount of jam in each depression.
5. Bake in the center of the oven for about 10 minutes or until
   lightly golden.

# cinnamon cookies

MAKES 50 COOKIES

1 batch of cookie dough, see basic
    recipe page 21
1/4 cup sugar
2 teaspoons ground cinnamon
1 beaten egg for brushing

1. Prepare the cookie dough according to the basic recipe.
2. Preheat the oven to 350°F.
3. Mix the sugar and the cinnamon.
4. Roll the dough into small balls and flatten them on a baking
   sheet lined with parchment paper.
5. Score across each cookie with a fork
6. Brush the cookies with beaten egg and sprinkle the sugar and
   cinnamon on top.
7. Bake in the center of the oven for about 10 minutes or until
   lightly golden.

# lovely toffee slices

This wicked recipe for wonderful, chewy toffee slices is a contribution from my little sister, Petronella. They are awesome!

MAKES 25 SLICES

1/2 cup unsalted butter, softened

1/3 cup sugar

3 tablespoons golden syrup or light corn syrup

1 1/4 cups all-purpose flour

1/2 teaspoon baking soda

1 teaspoon vanilla sugar

1 teaspoon ground ginger

1. Preheat the oven to 350°F.
2. Beat together the butter, sugar, and syrup until creamy.
3. Mix the flour, baking soda, vanilla sugar, and ginger and blend into the mixture.
4. Shape the dough into two long rolls.
5. Put the rolls on a baking sheet lined with parchment paper and flatten them slightly. Score each cookie with a fork.
6. Bake in the center of the oven for 12–15 minutes or until golden.
7. Let the rolls cool a bit before cutting them diagonally. Leave the toffee slices to cool completely on the baking sheet.

# hazelnut pyramids

When I bake hazelnut pyramids, I sometimes add some crushed coffee beans, or flavor the mixture with frangelico (hazelnut liquor). For that finishing touch I sometimes dip the bases in melted chocolate when the cakes have cooled. But they are lovely just the way they are, too! Remember that the smaller the pyramids, the shorter the time they need in the oven.

MAKES 16 PYRAMIDS

1/4 cup unsalted butter

1 cup plus 2 tablespoons hazelnuts

1/2 cup sugar

1 organic egg

hazelnuts for decoration

1. Preheat the oven to 350°F.
2. Melt the butter.
3. Process the hazelnuts in a blender to make a fine powder.
4. Mix the nuts with the butter, sugar, and egg.
5. Use your fingers to shape the mixture into pyramids on a baking sheet lined with parchment paper. Put one hazelnut on the top of each one.
6. Bake in the center of the oven for about 18 minutes or until golden. Leave them to cool completely on the baking sheet.

# lavender dream cookies

I invented these happy dreams on a rainy day in the countryside when I thought I wasn't using enough lavender in my cooking. You can also try making your own lavender sugar. It's really easy! Blend fresh lavender flowers with sugar in a jar. After about a week, the sugar will have absorbed the flavor. Superb for sprinkling on top of strawberries and vanilla ice cream.

**MAKES 20 COOKIES**

1/2 cup unsalted butter, softened

1/2 cup sugar

1 teaspoon vanilla sugar

1 1/2 cups all-purpose flour

1/2 teaspoon baking powder

1 tablespoon fresh or dried lavender flowers

1. Preheat the oven to 300°F.
2. Beat the butter and the sugar until pale and creamy.
3. Mix the dry ingredients with the lavender flowers and stir into the butter cream to make a crumbly dough.
4. Shape small balls and put them on a baking sheet lined with parchment paper.
5. Bake in the center of the oven for 15–20 minutes.

# oatmeal cookies

These crisp, wafer-thin cookies are a Swedish classic. I love eating them together with strawberries and ice cream in the summer. The recipe is perfect if you're cooking in an unfamiliar kitchen because it's so easy. Just mix the ingredients and pop the cookies in the oven. For a deluxe variation, dip half of each cookie in melted chocolate.

**MAKES 40 COOKIES**

1/2 cup plus 3 tablespoons unsalted butter

1 cup rolled oats

3/4 cup sugar

1/4 cup heavy whipping cream

1/4 cup golden syrup or light corn syrup

1 1/4 cups all-purpose flour

1/2 teaspoon baking powder

1. Preheat the oven to 400°F.
2. Melt the butter and mix with the rolled oats, sugar, heavy whipping cream and syrup in a bowl.
3. Mix the flour with the baking powder and fold into the mixture.
4. Use two teaspoons to drop the mixture onto a baking sheet lined with parchment paper. Leave about 4 in between the cookies because they will spread.
5. Bake in the center of the oven for about 4 minutes or until golden.

# on the cake plate

No garden party is complete without a good selection of splendid cakes. I am an absolute cake addict and adore these magnificent creations. In the following pages you'll find many of my favorite recipes for cherished classics, together with some inspiration from overseas, such as the New York-style Blueberry Cheesecake, Torta Della Nonna, and Plum Clafouti. I have tried out many variations over the years, and so I'm happy to share with you the recipes that I think are a cut above the rest. You have my word they will not disappoint your guests, whether they are stopping by for coffee or are devouring your creations at that indulgent garden party.

# nine juicy sponges

The trick to a spongy success is to beat the eggs and sugar until they are really fluffy. Never beat the flour into the mixture because that might give the sponge a rubber-like consistency. Instead, carefully fold the flour into the mixture. The basic recipe can be varied with all kinds of delicious flavorings (see below and pages 34-35).

MAKES 1 CAKE
BASIC RECIPE
3 organic eggs
1 cup sugar
1 teaspoon vanilla sugar
¼ cup unsalted butter
½ cup milk
2 cups all-purpose flour
2 teaspoons baking powder
1 pinch of salt
butter and dried breadcrumbs for the pan

1. Preheat the oven to 350°F.
2. Beat together the eggs, sugar, and vanilla sugar until white and fluffy.
3. Melt the butter and stir in milk. Mix into the egg mixture.
4. Mix the flour, baking powder, and salt. Carefully fold into the egg mixture.
5. Add a flavoring (see variations) or just pour the mixture into a buttered ring mold coated with breadcrumbs.
6. Bake in the center of the oven for 25–30 minutes or until a skewer inserted into the center comes out clean.
7. Leave the sponge to cool slightly in the pan and then turn it out onto a plate or a wire rack.

## old-style apple sponge

MAKES 1 CAKE
1 batch of sponge mixture, see basic recipe above
4 oz homemade almond paste, see page 208
butter and dried breadcrumbs for the pan

FILLING
2 large apples
2 tablespoons unsalted butter
3 tablespoons sugar
2 teaspoons ground cinnamon

1. Prepare the mixture according to the basic recipe and add the almond paste.
2. Core the apples and cut them into pieces. Fry the apples with the butter, sugar, and cinnamon until they start browning and soften.
3. Butter a ring mold and coat it with breadcrumbs. Mix the apples with the cake mixture and pour it into the mold.
4. Bake in the center of the preheated oven for 25–30 minutes or until a skewer inserted into the center comes out clean.
5. Leave the sponge to cool slightly in the pan and then turn it out onto a plate or a wire rack.

## blackcurrant sponge

MAKES 1 CAKE

1 batch of sponge mixture, see basic
    recipe page 30

1/2 cup buttermilk

zest and juice of 1 lemon

butter and dried breadcrumbs for the
    pan

FILLING

1 cup fresh or frozen blackcurrants

1 tablespoon all-purpose flour

1. Prepare the mixture according to the basic recipe, but replace
   the milk with buttermilk.
2. Mix the lemon zest and juice into the mixture.
3. Toss the blackcurrants in the flour. Shake off excess flour and
   add the currants and the mixture in layers to a buttered ring
   mold coated with breadcrumbs.
4. Bake in the center of the preheated oven for 25–30 minutes or
   until a skewer inserted into the center comes out clean.
5. Leave the sponge to cool in the pan and then turn it out onto a
   plate or a wire rack.

## cardamom sponge

MAKES 1 CAKE

1 batch of sponge mixture, see basic
    recipe page 30

1 tablespoon cardamom pods

butter and dried breadcrumbs for the
    pan

confectioner's sugar

1. Prepare the mixture according to the basic recipe, but add
   finely ground cardamom seeds to the milk and bring the milk
   to a boil before stirring it into the butter.
2. Pour into a buttered ring mold coated with breadcrumbs.
3. Bake in the center of the preheated oven for 25–30 minutes or
   until a skewer inserted into the center comes out clean.
4. Leave the sponge to cool in the pan and then turn it out onto a
   plate or a wire rack. Dust with confectioner's sugar before
   serving.

## amazing saffron sponge

MAKES 1 CAKE

1 batch of sponge mixture, see basic
    recipe page 30

1 pinch of saffron

1 tablespoon light rum

butter and unsweetened coconut for the
    pan

1. Prepare the mixture according to the basic recipe, but add the
   saffron to the milk and bring the milk to a boil before stirring
   it into the butter. Flavor the mixture with the rum.
2. Pour into a buttered ring mold coated with unsweetened coconut.
3. Bake in the center of the preheated oven for 25–30 minutes or
   until a skewer inserted into the center comes out clean.
4. Leave the sponge to cool in the pan and then turn it out onto a
   plate or a wire rack.

## soft gingerbread sponge

MAKES 1 CAKE

1 batch of sponge mixture,
    see basic recipe page 30

1/2 cup buttermilk

1 teaspoon ground ginger

2 teaspoons ground cinnamon

2 teaspoons ground clove

zest of 1 orange

butter and slivered almonds for the pan

1. Prepare the mixture according to the basic recipe, but replace
   the milk with buttermilk. Add the spices and orange zest.
2. Pour into a buttered ring mold coated with slivered almonds.
3. Bake in the center of the preheated oven for 25–30 minutes or
   until a skewer inserted into the center comes out clean.
4. Leave the sponge to cool in the pan and then turn it out on to
   a plate or a wire rack.

## lemon poppy seed sponge

MAKES 1 CAKE

1 batch of sponge mixture, see basic
    recipe page 30
zest of 3 lemons
juice of 1 lemon
3 ½ tablespoons poppy seeds

LEMON ICING

2 ½ cups confectioner's sugar
¼ cup plus 2 tablespoons freshly
    squeezed lemon juice
butter and dried breadcrumbs for the
    pan

1. Prepare the mixture according to the basic recipe and add the
   lemon zest and juice and the poppy seeds.
2. Pour into a buttered ring mold coated with breadcrumbs.
3. Bake in the center of the preheated oven for 25–30 minutes or
   until a skewer inserted into the center comes out clean.
4. Leave the sponge to cool in the pan and then turn it out on to
   a plate or a wire rack.
5. Mix together the confectioner's sugar and lemon juice until
   smooth, then drizzle the icing over the sponge.

## coconut tosca sponge

MAKES 1 CAKE

1 batch of sponge mixture, see basic
    recipe page 30
butter and dried breadcrumbs for the
    pan

CRUNCHY TOP

2 tablespoons butter
¼ cup light syrup
1 ¼ cups unsweetened coconut
¼ cup sugar

1. Prepare the mixture according to the basic recipe. Butter a
   9-inch springform cake pan and coat with breadcrumbs.
2. Pour in the mixture. Bake in the center of the preheated oven
   for about 25 minutes.
3. In the meantime, prepare the crunchy top. Stir together the
   ingredients for the topping in a saucepan. Bring to a boil and
   boil for about 5 minutes.
4. Remove the cake from the oven and cover the sponge with the
   crunchy top. Return the cake to the oven and bake for another
   15 minutes or until the topping is golden.
5. Leave the sponge to cool before removing the sides of the
   springform cake pan.

## strawberry & rhubarb sponge

MAKES 1 CAKE

zest of 2 limes
juice of 1 lime
butter and dried breadcrumbs for the
    pan

FILLING

½ cup fresh strawberries
1 large rhubarb stick
¼ cup confectioner's sugar
1 tablespoon all-purpose flour

1. Prepare the mixture according to the basic recipe. Add the
   lime zest and juice to the mixture.
2. Cut the strawberries and the rhubarb into thin slices and
   blend them with the confectioner's sugar and flour. Add to the
   cake mixture.
3. Pour the mixture into a buttered ring mold coated with
   breadcrumbs.
4. Bake in the center of the preheated oven for 25–30 minutes or
   until a skewer inserted into the center comes out clean.
5. Leave the sponge to cool in the pan and then turn it out on to a
   plate or a wire rack.

# chocolate chip walnut brownies

A brownie should have a moist and creamy texture. I learned this recipe when I worked at a French patisserie in Stockholm. Serve it either as a coffee break treat or as a dessert together with softened vanilla ice cream.

MAKES 12 BROWNIES

1 ½ cups unsalted butter, softened

2 ¼ cups sugar

⅓ cup good-quality cocoa powder

⅓ cup golden syrup or light corn syrup

6 organic eggs, beaten

1 ¾ cups all-purpose flour

14 oz good-quality white chocolate

1 cup walnuts

walnuts for decoration

FUDGE GLAZE

1 cup whipping cream

⅓ cup milk

⅓ cup golden syrup or light corn syrup

1 teaspoon ground ginger

14 oz good-quality dark chocolate (70% cocoa solids)

1. Preheat the oven to 350°F.
2. Mix the butter and the sugar until pale and creamy.
3. Stir in the cocoa powder and syrup.
4. Mix in the eggs one at a time, and then carefully add the flour into the mixture.
5. Chop the chocolate coarsely and blend into the mixture together with the chopped walnuts.
6. Line a square cake pan, 9 x 13 in, with parchment paper. Pour in the mixture.
7. Bake in the center of the oven for 15–25 minutes or until a skewer inserted into the center comes out slightly sticky.
8. Leave the cake to cool.
9. Bring the cream, milk, syrup, and ginger to a boil. Take the saucepan off the heat.
10. Chop the chocolate finely and blend it into the warm mixture. Stir until the chocolate melts.
11. Spread the glaze over the cake and sprinkle over a few whole walnuts. Leave in the fridge until set. Cut the cake in squares.

# plum clafouti

This eggy French pudding is best served at room temperature accompanied with softened vanilla ice cream and lightly whipped cream. The pudding is easy to vary with all kinds of fresh berries. Just sprinkle the berries into the mixture, without frying. The clafouti also tastes really good made with apples, pears, or rhubarb. Cut these fruits into pieces or slices and fry them like the plums.

**MAKES 1 CAKE**

8 ripe plums
2 ½ tablespoons unsalted butter
2 tablespoons (superfine) sugar
1 teaspoon ground cinnamon
butter and sugar for the pan
slivered almonds to decorate

**CLAFOUTI MIXTURE**

½ cup slivered almonds
½ vanilla pod
¼ cup all-purpose flour
¼ cup sugar
zest of 1 lime
1 cup whipping cream
2 organic eggs
2 organic egg yolks

1. Preheat the oven to 350°F.
2. Halve and pit the plums. Fry them, cut side down in the butter, sugar, and cinnamon. Leave to cool.
3. Make the clafouti. Grind the almonds in a blender to make a fine powder.
4. Split the vanilla pod lengthways and scrape out the seeds. Mix together the almond powder, flour, sugar, and lime zest.
5. Add the cream, eggs, and egg yolks and beat until smooth.
6. Butter a 2 quart casserole dish and sprinkle with sugar. Pour in the mixture.
7. Arrange the plums, cut side up, in the dish and sprinkle over the slivered almonds.
8. Bake in the center of the oven for 35–40 minutes or until golden and the mixture is set.

# speedy berry cake

I have spent many summer days in the Stockholm archipelago, where some friends have a summer cottage. Summertime is berry cake time. Try this delicious quick and easy cake, which can be varied with all kinds of different berries.

**MAKES 1 CAKE**

½ cup plus 1 tablespoon butter

⅔ cup sugar

1 ¼ cups all-purpose flour

1 ½ teaspoons baking powder

1 pinch of salt

1 organic egg

½ cup fresh or frozen berries

1 tablespoon all-purpose flour

butter and dried breadcrumbs for the pan

1. Preheat the oven to 350°F.
2. Bring the butter and the sugar to a boil and simmer for 1 minute. Leave to cool.
3. Mix together the flour, baking powder, and salt and fold into the butter mixture. Stir in the egg.
4. Pour the mixture into a buttered 9 in springform cake pan covered with breadcrumbs or a small ovenproof dish.
5. Toss the berries in the flour, shake off any excess, and sprinkle the berries over the cake.
6. Bake in the center of the oven for about 20 minutes or until golden.

# pecan banana bread

This incredibly moist cake is a wonderful treat at a coffee break. It is delicious for dessert as well, especially if you toast the slices in a dry frying pan. Like toast with ice cream!

MAKES 1 CAKE

2/3 cup unsalted butter, softened

1/3 cup sugar

1 cup confectioner's sugar

4 ripe bananas

2 organic eggs

1 3/4 cups all-purpose flour

1 teaspoon baking powder

1/2 teaspoon ground cinnamon

1/2 teaspoon ground ginger

1 pinch of salt

2/3 cup pecan nuts

butter and dried breadcrumbs for the pan

1. Preheat the oven to 350°F.
2. Beat together the butter, sugar, and confectioner's sugar until pale and creamy.
3. Mash the bananas and stir them into the mixture. Beat in the eggs.
4. Mix the dry ingredients with the whole pecan nuts (reserving a few to sprinkle on top of the cake) and carefully blend into the mixture.
5. Pour the mixture into a buttered rectangular loaf pan covered with breadcrumbs and bake in the center of the oven for about 30 minutes or until a skewer inserted into the center comes out clean.

# semolina cake with cherries

A friend of mine gave me the recipe for this crunchy and rather special cake. His mother bakes it, and he always tells me it is the best cake ever.

MAKES 1 CAKE

3/4 cup sugar

2 organic eggs

2/3 cup unsalted butter, softened

1 1/2 cups all-purpose flour

1 pinch of salt

1/3 cup semolina flour

1 3/4 cups fresh or canned cherries, drained and pitted

butter and dried breadcrumbs for the pan

1. Preheat the oven to 400°F.
2. Beat together the sugar and the eggs until pale and fluffy.
3. Mix in the butter.
4. Mix together the flour, salt, and semolina and blend into the mixture.
5. Pour the mixture into a buttered 9 in springform cake pan covered with breadcrumbs. Lightly press the cherries into the mixture.
6. Bake in the center of the oven for 25–30 minutes or until a skewer inserted into the center comes out clean.

# chocolate darlings

The best recipes are passed down from generation to generation, and I've borrowed this one from my mum's recipe book. These moist and fluffy cakes are a Swedish classic.

MAKES 1 CAKE
5 organic eggs
1 ⅓ cups sugar
2 ¾ cups all-purpose flour
3 teaspoons baking powder
1 pinch of salt
¼ cup plus 2 tablespoons good-quality cocoa powder
¾ cup water
1 ¼ cups plus 2 tablespoons unsalted butter, melted
7 oz good-quality dark chocolate, (70% cocoa solids)
1 ¼ cups unsweetened coconut

CHOCOLATE ICING
¾ cup plus 2 tablespoons whipping cream
3 tablespoons espresso coffee
7 oz good-quality dark chocolate (70% cocoa solids)

1. Preheat the oven to 400°F.
2. Beat together the eggs and the sugar until they are pale and fluffy.
3. Mix together the dry ingredients and carefully blend into the egg mixture.
4. Add the water and melted butter and stir to combine.
5. Line an 8 x 8 in cake pan with parchment paper. Pour the mixture into the pan.
6. Sprinkle coarsely chopped chocolate over the top.
7. Bake in the center of the oven for 10–15 minutes or until a skewer inserted into the center comes out slightly sticky. Leave to cool.
8. Bring the whipping cream to a boil, stir in the coffee, and leave to cool slightly.
9. Finely chop the chocolate, add the cream, and stir until melted. Spread the icing over the cake.
10. Sprinkle coconut on top and leave to set.
11. Cut into squares.

# new york blueberry cheesecake

This is a wonderful original recipe from a diner in New York. I love this cake, and even my American friend says it's the best cheesecake ever. It's also very easy to make. The cake is easier to cut if you serve it chilled. If the cake gets stuck in the pan, use a small knife to run around the edge to loosen it.

MAKES 1 CAKE

CRUST

3 cups vanilla wafer cookies

½ cup plus 2 tablespoons unsalted butter, melted


5 oz cream cheese

1 cup cottage cheese

⅓ cup sugar

¼ cup cornstarch

2 teaspoons vanilla sugar

3 organic eggs

⅓ cup heavy whipping cream

7 oz good-quality white chocolate

¾ cup fresh or frozen blueberries

1. Preheat the oven to 350°F.
2. Grind the cookies finely in a blender and mix the crumbs with the melted butter.
3. Press the mixture into the bottom of a nonstick 9 in springform cake pan.
4. Bake in the center of the oven for about 10 minutes. Leave to cool.
5. Beat together the cream cheese and curd cheese until creamy.
6. Mix together the sugar, cornstarch, and vanilla sugar and add to the cheese mixture.
7. Beat in the eggs, one at a time, and then fold in the whipping cream.
8. Break the chocolate into pieces and melt in a bowl set over a pan of simmering water. Stir the chocolate into the cheesecake filling.
9. Pour the filling over the crust and sprinkle the blueberries on top.
10. Bake in the center of the oven for about 40 minutes. To prevent the cheesecake from browning, cover it with foil when it is golden brown.
11. Turn off the oven and leave the cheesecake to continue cooking in the residual heat for 30 minutes.

# the best carrot cake ever

You can find an almost infinite number of variations of this moist American cake, but this is definitely the best one I have ever tried.

MAKES 1 CAKE

3 organic eggs

1 ¼ cups sugar

1 ¾ cups all-purpose flour

1 teaspoon vanilla sugar

1 tablespoon baking powder

1 ½ teaspoons ground cinnamon

1 teaspoon ground cardamom

½ teaspoon ground ginger

1 pinch of salt

½ cup plus 2 tablespoons sunflower oil

1 lb carrots, grated

butter and dried breadcrumbs for the pan

CREAM CHEESE LIME FROSTING

¼ cup plus 1 tablespoon unsalted butter, softened

2 cups confectioner's sugar

1 teaspoon vanilla sugar

zest of 1 lime

½ cup cream cheese

1. Preheat the oven to 300°F.
2. Beat together the eggs and the sugar until pale and fluffy.
3. Mix together all the dry ingredients and blend into the egg mixture.
4. Stir in the oil and carrots.
5. Pour the mixture into a buttered 9 in springform cake pan covered with breadcrumbs.
6. Bake in the center of the oven for about 55 minutes or until a skewer inserted into the center comes out clean.
7. Leave the cake to cool.
8. Mix together the ingredients for the frosting until creamy and smooth, then spread the frosting over the top of the cake.

# torta della nonna

Torta della nonna means granny's cake, and it is an Italian cheesecake with almonds, egg, and cream cheese. It's usually quite complicated to make, but I have made my own simple version. I like to serve it with lightly whipped cream.

MAKES 1 CAKE

½ cup plus 2 tablespoons unsalted butter, softened

11 oz homemade almond paste, see recipe page 208

6 organic eggs

1 cup ricotta cheese

zest of 1 lemon

zest of 1 orange

1 teaspoon almond extract

¼ cup all-purpose flour

butter and slivered almonds for the pan

pine nuts

confectioner's sugar

1. Preheat the oven to 350°F.
2. Mix together the butter and the grated almond paste until creamy.
3. Add the eggs, one at a time, beating to make a smooth mixture.
4. Stir in the cheese, citrus zest, and almond extract. Fold in the flour.
5. Butter a 9 in springform cake pan and cover with crushed slivered almonds.
6. Pour in the mixture and sprinkle pine nuts over the top.
7. Bake in the center of the oven for 25–30 minutes or until a skewer inserted into the center comes out clean.
8. Dust confectioner's sugar over the cake before serving.

# sticky chocolate cake

Everyone's got their own favorite version of this simple, yet incredibly addictive, Swedish classic. I like mine both toffeelike and sticky, and here's my best recipe.

MAKES 1 CAKE

¼ cup unsalted butter

¼ cup vegetable oil

2 organic eggs

¾ cup sugar

⅓ cup brown sugar

1 ½ cups all-purpose flour

5 tablespoons good-quality cocoa powder

2 teaspoons baking powder

1 teaspoon vanilla sugar

1 pinch of salt

butter and dried breadcrumbs for the pan

2 oz good-quality dark chocolate (70% cocoa solids)

1. Preheat the oven to 300°F.
2. Melt the butter in a saucepan. Add the oil.
3. Beat together the eggs and sugars until pale and fluffy. Stir in the hot butter.
4. Mix together the dry ingredients and blend into the mixture.
5. Butter a 9 in springform cake pan and cover it with breadcrumbs. Pour the mixture into the pan. Break the chocolate into pieces and add to the mixture.
6. Bake in the center of the oven for about 30 minutes or until a skewer inserted into the center comes out slightly sticky.

# tarts, flans & pies

These recipes are some of my friends' big favorites, and they have a place in my heart too. Some are old classics and some are new ideas. If you are in a hurry, I can recommend The Apple Lady's Crumble, Easy-to-make French Fruit Flan, or Strawberry Flan with Toffee Cream. If you like being well-prepared, take a look at the Royale Pies which are really practical because you can freeze them unbaked and then stick them straight in the oven when your guests are on their way: not just really tasty but efficient too!

# classic shortcrust pastry dough

When you make shortcrust pastry dough, don't knead it too much or it will turn dense and lose its crustiness. You can easily make a chocolate shortcrust pastry dough by adding 2 tablespoons of cocoa powder.

MAKES ENOUGH FOR 2 TARTS
BASIC RECIPE

²/₃ cup cold unsalted butter, diced

2 ¹/₃ cup all-purpose flour

¹/₄ cup confectioner's sugar

1 organic egg, beaten

¹/₂ tablespoon cold water

1. Put the butter, flour, and sugar in a bowl and mix with your fingertips to make a mixture that resembles wet sand.
2. Add the egg and the water and gently work the dough to bind the ingredients together. Don't knead.
3. Cover with plastic wrap and leave to rest in the refrigerator for 30 minutes.

# classic crumble

This crumble mix can be kept in the refrigerator for a few days. Then all you have to do is take it out of the fridge when you want to sprinkle it over a pie.

MAKES ENOUGH FOR 1 PIE
BASIC RECIPE

¹/₂ cup cold unsalted butter, diced

¹/₂ cup plus 2 tablespoons all-purpose flour

¹/₄ cup (superfine) sugar

¹/₄ cup slivered almonds

³/₄ cup rolled oats

1. Put the butter, flour, and sugar in a bowl and mix with your fingertips to make a mixture that resembles wet sand.
2. Mix the slivered almonds and rolled oats into the breadcrumbs.

# oat pastry dough

Pies made with an oat pastry dough are really lovely! Don't bake them for too long because the pastry easily turns hard. It's ready when it starts to turn light brown.

MAKES ENOUGH FOR 1 PIE
BASIC RECIPE

³/₄ cup unsalted butter, softened

³/₄ cup all-purpose flour

¹/₂ cup sugar

³/₄ cup rolled oats

1. Preheat the oven to 350°F.
2. Melt the butter and stir in the flour, sugar, and rolled oats.
3. Press the dough into a pie tin.
4. Prebake in the center of the oven for about 15 minutes.

# french royale in nine ways

This pie is both super tasty and really practical because you can make it complete with crust and filling and freeze it uncooked. Then all you have to do is take the pie out of the freezer and put it in the oven. It's a perfect surprise when friends come over unexpectedly or to serve as a dessert if you want to prepare it in advance for a party.

MAKES 1 PIE/SERVES 8

BASIC RECIPE

1 batch of classic shortcrust pastry
   dough, see basic recipe page 55

ROYALE MIXTURE

4 oz homemade almond paste, see
   recipe page 208
3 organic eggs
1 cup cottage cheese
1/3 cup crème fraiche
1/3 cup sugar
filling (see variations)

1. Prepare the shortcrust pastry according to the basic recipe.
2. Preheat the oven to 350°F.
3. Roll out the dough and use it to line a tart pan.
4. Grate the almond paste and mix it with the other ingredients for the royale mixture.
5. Flavor with a filling of your choice (see below) and bake for 30-40 minutes in the oven.

## berry royale

MAKES 1 PIE/SERVES 8

1 prepared French royale with mixture,
   see basic recipe above
3/4 cup mixed fresh or frozen berries
1 handful of slivered almonds

1. Spread the berries on top of the pie and sprinkle with the slivered almonds.
2. Bake in the lower part of the preheated oven for 30–40 minutes or until golden and the mixture is set (or put the prepared pie in the freezer and bake it on another occasion).

## fig royale

MAKES 1 PIE/SERVES 8

1 prepared French royale with mixture,
   see basic recipe above
8 ripe figs
2 1/2 tablespoons unsalted butter
3 tablespoons sugar
2 teaspoons ground cinnamon
1 handful of slivered almonds

1. Split the figs in half and cut off the stems. Fry, cut side down, in a pan with the butter, sugar, and cinnamon for about 3 minutes.
2. Spread the figs over the pie with cut side up. Sprinkle with the slivered almonds.
3. Bake in the lower part of the preheated oven for 30–40 minutes or until golden and the mixture is set (or put the prepared pie in the freezer and bake it on another occasion).

## blackberry & lemon royale

MAKES 1 PIE/SERVES 8

1 prepared French royale with mixture,
    see basic recipe page 56
zest of 2 lemons
1 ½ cups fresh or frozen blackberries
1 handful of slivered almonds

1. Spread the lemon zest and blackberries over the pie. Sprinkle with the slivered almonds.
2. Bake in the lower part of the preheated oven for 30–40 minutes or until golden and the mixture is set (or put the prepared pie in the freezer and bake it on another occasion).

## nectarine royale

MAKES 1 PIE/SERVES 8

1 prepared French royale with mixture,
    see basic recipe page 56
4 ripe nectarines
1 handful of slivered almonds

1. Halve the nectarines and remove the pits. Cut the flesh into thin slices.
2. Arrange the nectarines over the pie. Sprinkle with the slivered almonds.
3. Bake in the lower part of the preheated oven for 30–40 minutes or until golden and the mixture is set (or put the prepared pie in the freezer and bake it on another occasion).

## red currant royale

MAKES 1 PIE/SERVES 8

1 prepared French royale with mixture,
    see basic recipe page 56
1 ½ cups fresh or frozen redcurrants
    (or blueberries or cranberries,
    chopped)
1 handful of slivered almonds

1. Spread the red currants over the pie. Sprinkle with the slivered almonds.
2. Bake in the lower part of the preheated oven for 30–40 minutes or until golden and the mixture is set (or put the prepared pie in the freezer and bake it on another occasion).

## plum royale

MAKES 1 PIE/SERVES 8

1 prepared French royale with mixture,
    see basic recipe page 56
6 ripe plums
2 ½ tablespoons unsalted butter
2 tablespoons sugar
2 teaspoons ground cinnamon
1 handful of slivered almonds

1. Halve the plums and remove the pits.
2. Melt the butter, sugar, and cinnamon in a frying pan and cook the plums, cut side down, for about 3 minutes.
3. Spread the plums, cut side up, over the pie. Sprinkle with the slivered almonds.
4. Bake in the lower part of the preheated oven for 30–40 minutes or until golden and the mixture is set (or put the prepared pie in the freezer and bake it on another occasion).

## apricot royale

MAKES 1 PIE/SERVES 8

1 prepared French royale with mixture,
    see basic recipe page 56
8 ripe apricots
2 ½ tablespoons unsalted butter
3 tablespoons sugar
2 teaspoons ground cinnamon
1 teaspoon cardamom
1 handful of slivered almonds

1. Halve the apricots and remove the pits.
2. Melt the butter, sugar, cinnamon, and cardamom in a frying pan and cook the apricots, cut side down, for about 3 minutes.
3. Spread the apricots, cut side up, over the pie. Sprinkle with the slivered almonds.
4. Bake in the lower part of the preheated oven for 30–40 minutes or until golden and the mixture is set (or put the prepared pie in the freezer and bake it on another occasion).

## pear royale

MAKES 1 PIE/SERVES 8

1 prepared French royale with mixture,
    see basic recipe page 56
8 canned pear halves
1 handful of slivered almonds

1. Drain the pears and put them, cut side down, on a chopping-board. Slice the halves lengthways and press down gently to spread them like a fan.
2. Arrange the fans, cut side down, over the pie. Sprinkle with the slivered almonds.
3. Bake in the lower part of the preheated oven for 30–40 minutes or until golden and the mixture is set (or put the prepared pie in the freezer and bake it on another occasion).

## raspberry royale with lime

MAKES 1 PIE/SERVES 8

1 prepared French royale with mixture,
    see basic recipe page 56
zest of 2 limes
1 ¼ cups fresh or frozen raspberries
1 handful of slivered almonds

1. Spread the lime zest and raspberries over the pie. Sprinkle with the slivered almonds.
2. Bake in the lower part of the preheated oven for 30–40 minutes or until golden and the mixture is set (or put the prepared pie in the freezer and bake it on another occasion).

# nutty fig tart

This recipe is a contribution from an Italian friend. The pie is irresistibly nutty, and I like to serve it with softened vanilla ice cream or lightly whipped cream. When you are buying chocolate, keep an eye on the cocoa content. I like to use chocolate containing 70% cocoa solids when baking. The high cocoa content gives a rich taste but without the bitterness that chocolate exceeding 70% sometimes has. I never use cooking chocolate because the quality is too low, and it also contains a lot of unnecessary additives.

MAKES 1 PIE/SERVES 10

1 batch of classic shortcrust pastry
    dough, see basic recipe page 55

FILLING

1 ½ cups almonds

1 ¼ cups plus 2 tablespoons unsalted
    butter, softened

1 cup sugar

3 organic eggs

zest of 1 orange

²/₃ cup all-purpose flour

5 oz good quality dark chocolate (70%
    cocoa solids)

8–10 fresh figs

1. Prepare the shortcrust pastry according to the basic recipe. Roll out the dough and use it to line a tart pan.
2. Preheat the oven to 350°F.
3. Blanch the almonds and grind in a blender to make a fine powder.
4. Beat the butter and the sugar until pale and creamy.
5. Stir in the orange zest. Add the eggs one at a time, beating the mixture after each addition.
6. Carefully blend the almond powder and flour into the egg mixture. Add the coarsely chopped chocolate.
7. Pour the mixture into the pan.
8. Cut a cross in the tops of some of the figs and open them out slightly to reveal the seeds. Cut the remaining figs into pieces. Add all the figs to the mixture.
9. Bake in the lower part of the oven for about 55 minutes or until golden and the mixture is set.

# american apple pie

Shortcrust pastry dough should be handled as little as possible. All the ingredients should be cold and hold together just enough to form a dough. You can make the dough in advance and keep it in the freezer or line the pie plate with the pastry and freeze the whole thing, which makes it easier when you have a sudden urge to make a pie. There are several ways to avoid the edges from sliding down when you prebake the pastry shell. I usually prop them up with tin foil, but just make sure that the foil is stuck on hard enough. You can also fill the pastry shell with dried beans. For this recipe you don't need to prebake the pastry.

MAKES 1 PIE/SERVES 8

1 batch of classic shortcrust pastry
    dough, see basic recipe page 55
egg and milk for brushing
demerara sugar

FILLING

12 big Granny Smith apples
juice of 1 lemon
¼ cup butter
5 tablespoons sugar
2 teaspoons ground cinnamon
1 teaspoon ground ginger

1. Prepare the shortcrust pastry according to the basic recipe.
2. Preheat the oven to 350°F.
3. Core and slice the apples and put them in a bowl with the lemon juice.
4. Melt the butter in a frying pan. Add the sugar, cinnamon, and ginger and fry the apples. You will find it easier to do this in two batches. Transfer the apples to a plate to cool.
5. Divide the dough into two pieces, one a bit bigger than the other.
6. Put the larger piece of dough on a lightly floured surface and roll it out to a circle about 12 in across.
7. Supporting the pastry on your rolling pin, use it to line a 9 in pie plate. Press the pastry gently against the bottom and sides of the pie plate, leaving the excess hanging over the edge.
8. Fill the pastry case with the fried apples.
9. Roll out the smaller piece of pastry to a circle about 10 in across.
10. Beat an egg with a splash of milk and brush the edges of the pastry. Put the top crust on top of the pie.
11. Pinch the pastry discs firmly together and trim away excess pastry hanging over the sides.
12. Put the pie plate on a baking sheet, brush the top with the egg mixture, and sprinkle over demerara sugar. Make slits (to make sunbeams) or pinch small holes in the top crust. Bake in the lower part of the oven for about 35 minutes or until golden.

# the apple lady's crumble

When I was young, we used to steal apples from the Apple Lady. I named this tasty crumble pie after her. Serve the pie with lightly whipped cream or speedy vanilla custard (see page 208).

MAKES 1 BIG PIE/4 SMALL PIES
BASIC RECIPE
1 cup plus 2 tablespoons cold unsalted butter, diced
1 1/4 cups demerara sugar
1 cup unsweetened coconut
1 1/4 cups all-purpose flour
3/4 cup rolled oats

1. Put the butter in a bowl. Add the sugar, coconut, and flour and mix lightly with your fingertips to make a mixture that resembles wet sand.
2. Carefully blend in the rolled oats without breaking them.
3. Add the filling of your choice (see below), then bake for about 25 minutes.

## blueberry crumble

MAKES 1 BIG PIE/4 SMALL PIES
1 batch of Apple Lady's Crumble, see basic recipe above
butter for the dish and to dot on top of the pie

FILLING
4 cups fresh or frozen blueberries
zest of 2 lemons
1 1/4 cups sugar
3 tablespoons cornstarch

1. Prepare the crumble according to the basic recipe.
2. Preheat the oven to 400°F.
3. Mix the blueberries, lemon zest, sugar, and cornstarch in a bowl.
4. Cover the bottom of a buttered ovenproof dish with the berries. Spread the crumble over the top and dot with some butter.
5. Bake in the center of the preheated oven for about 25 minutes or until golden.

## cherry crumble

MAKES 1 BIG PIE/4 SMALL PIES
1 batch of Apple Lady's Crumble, see basic recipe above
butter for the dish and to dot on top of the pie

FILLING
3 cups fresh cherries
zest of 1 orange
1/3 cup dark muscovado sugar
3 tablespoons cornstarch

1. Prepare the crumble according to the basic recipe.
2. Preheat the oven to 400°F.
3. Pit the cherries and mix them with the orange zest, sugar, and cornstarch in a bowl.
4. Cover the bottom of a buttered ovenproof dish with the cherries. Spread the crumble over the top and dot with some butter.
5. Bake in the center of the preheated oven for about 25 minutes or until golden.

## strawberry & rhubarb crumble

**MAKES 1 BIG PIE/4 SMALL PIES**

1 batch of crumble, see basic recipe
    page 69

butter for the dish and to dot on top of
    the pie

**FILLING**

3 large rhubarb sticks

1 ¼ cups fresh strawberries

4 pieces of crystallized ginger

⅓ cup sugar

3 tablespoons cornstarch

1. Prepare the crumble according to the basic recipe.
2. Preheat the oven to 400°F.
3. Wash and chop the rhubarb, removing any stringy bits. Hull and halve the strawberries.
4. Finely chop the ginger and mix it with the rhubarb, strawberries, sugar, and cornstarch.
5. Cover the bottom of a buttered ovenproof dish with the fruit. Spread the crumble over the top and dot with butter.
6. Bake in the center of the preheated oven for about 25 minutes or until golden.

## peach & apple crumble

**MAKES 1 BIG PIE/4 SMALL PIES**

1 batch of crumble, see basic recipe
    page 69

butter for the dish and to dot on top of
    the pie

**FILLING**

4 ripe cooking apples

4 ripe nectarines

2 ½ tablespoons unsalted butter

3 tablespoons sugar

2 teaspoons ground cinnamon

2 teaspoons ground ginger

1. Prepare the crumble according to the basic recipe.
2. Preheat the oven to 400°F.
3. Cut the fruit into pieces and fry (in batches if necessary) in the butter, sugar, and spices.
4. Cover the bottom of a buttered ovenproof dish with the fruit. Spread the crumble over the top and dot with butter.
5. Bake in the center of the preheated oven for about 25 minutes or until golden.

## my garden crumble

**MAKES 1 BIG PIE/4 SMALL PIES**

1 batch of crumble, see basic recipe
    page 69

butter for the dish and to dot on top of
    the pie

**FILLING**

4 cups mixed fresh garden berries

⅓ cup sugar

1 tablespoon cornstarch

1. Prepare the crumble according to the basic recipe.
2. Preheat the oven to 400°F.
3. Mix the berries with the sugar and cornstarch in a bowl.
4. Cover the bottom of a buttered ovenproof dish with the berries. Spread the crumble over the top and dot with butter.
5. Bake in the center of the preheated oven for about 25 minutes or until golden.

# crunchy blueberry pie

Nothing can compare with my granny's wonderful blueberry pie. I just love this recipe!

MAKES 1 PIE/SERVES 8

1 batch of classic shortcrust pastry
   dough or oat pastry dough,
   see recipe page 55

FILLING

2 1/4 cups fresh or frozen blueberries

1 cup blueberry jam

1 tablespoon balsamic vinegar

3 tablespoons cornstarch

CRUNCHY TOPPING

1/4 cup plus 2 tablespoons unsalted
   butter

1 cup rolled oats

1/2 cup sugar

1. Prepare the pastry according to the basic recipe.
2. Preheat the oven to 350°F.
3. Roll out the pastry on a lightly floured board into a circle and use it to line a pie plate or tart pan. Prick the base with a fork. Fill the case with foil or beans and prebake in the oven for about 10 minutes.
4. Make the filling by mixing together the blueberries, jam, and vinegar. Stir in the cornstarch and pour the mixture into the pastry case.
5. Make the topping by melting the butter. Stir in the oats and sugar and leave to stand for 2-3 minutes.
6. Sprinkle the topping over the filling and bake in the center of the oven for about 25 minutes or until golden.

# butterscotch pecan pie

This pie is good all year round, summer as well as at Christmas! If you'd like to vary the flavoring you can add some ginger or cardamom. To check if the butterscotch is ready, drop a little of the mixture into a glass of really cold water. If it hardens a little so that you can form a soft, little ball it is ready and will set in the pie. I allow the pie to come to room temperature before serving, because keeping it in the fridge makes the filling a bit hard. Serve the pie accompanied by Raspberry Fool Cream (see page 211).

MAKES 1 PIE/SERVES 8

1 batch of classic shortcrust pastry
   dough or oat pastry dough,
   see recipe page 55
2 handfuls of pecan nuts

FILLING

1 vanilla pod
2 1/4 cups whipping cream
1 1/4 cups sugar
3 tablespoons brown sugar
3 tablespoons honey
1/2 cup golden syrup
1 tablespoon good-quality cocoa powder
1/4 cup unsalted butter, softened

1. Prepare the dough according to the basic recipe.
2. Preheat the oven to 350°F.
3. Roll out the pastry on a lightly floured surface into a circle and use it to line a pie plate or tart pan. Prick the base with a fork. Fill the case with foil or beans and prebake for about 10 minutes.
4. Split the vanilla pod lengthways and scrape out the seeds.
5. Put all ingredients except the butter in a saucepan. Heat, then simmer for about an hour.
6. Use the cold water test described above. When the butterscotch is ready, stir in the butter in pieces.
7. Fill the pie shell with butterscotch, sprinkle whole pecans on top, and put in the refrigerator to set.

# conversion chart

The measurements in this book have been converted to units more commonly used in the United States. Should you prefer to use scales, this chart will prove helpful. These are not always exact equivalents but are rounded up or down for convenient measuring. Only use one set of measurements in a recipe, do not mix the two.

SOLID MEASURES

| ounces | pounds | grams |
|---|---|---|
| ¼ | | 5 |
| ½ | | 15 |
| ¾ | | 20 |
| 1 | | 25 |
| 1 ¼ | | 30 |
| 1 ½ | | 40 |
| 2 | | 50 |
| 2 ⅓ | | 60 |
| 2 ½ | | 65 |
| 2 ⅔ | | 70 |
| 3 | | 75 |
| 3 ½ | | 90 |
| 4 | ¼ | 100 |
| 4 ¼ | | 110 |
| 4 ½ | | 120 |
| 4 ¾ | | 135 |
| 5 | | 150 |
| 6 | | 175 |
| 6 ¼ | | 180 |
| 7 | | 200 |
| 7 ½ | | 210 |
| 8 | ½ | 225 |
| 8½ | | 240 |
| 9 | | 250 |
| 9 ½ | | 270 |
| 10 | | 280 |
| 11 | | 300 |
| 12 | ¾ | 350 |
| 14 | | 400 |
| 15 | | 420 |
| 16 | 1 | 450 |
| 18 | | 500 |
| 20 | 1 ¼ | 550 |
| 24 | 1 ½ | 675 |
| 28 | 1 ¾ | 800 |
| 32 | 2 | 900 |
| 36 | 2 ¼ | 1 kg |
| 40 | 3 ½ | 2 kg |

LIQUID MEASURES

| fluid ounces | imperial | millilitres |
|---|---|---|
| | 1 teaspoon | 5 |
| | 1 dessertspoon | 10 |
| | 1 tablespoon | 15 |
| 1 | 2 tablespoons | 25 |
| 2 | | 50 |
| 3 | | 75 |
| 3 ½ | | 100 |
| 4 | | 110 |
| 5 | ¼ pint | 150 |
| 6 | | 170 |
| 7 | | 200 |
| 8 | | 250 |
| 10 | ½ pint | 300 |
| 14 | | 400 |
| 15 | ¾ pint | 450 |
| 17 | | 500 |
| 25 | 1 ¼ pints | 750 |
| 30 | 1 ½ pints | 900 |
| 50 | 2 ½ pints | 1.5 litres |

# easy-to-make french fruit flan

I often vary this delicious recipe to make flans with fresh apples, nectarines, plums, or apricots. You can also make them with canned peaches or apricots.

MAKES 8 FLANS

8 pieces of puff pasty, 4 x 8 in, thawed if frozen

egg for brushing

5 oz homemade almond paste, see recipe page 208 (or use store-bought marzipan)

4–5 ripe pears or peaches

1/2 cup demerara sugar

2 teaspoons ground cinnamon

4 sprigs of fresh rosemary

1 handful of slivered almonds

cold butter to slice on top of the flans

confectioner's sugar

1. Preheat the oven to 400°F.
2. Use a glass to mark two circles in each pastry sheet, but not all the way through. Use a fork to prick the surface of the circles.
3. Brush the edges of the circles with beaten egg.
4. Grate the almond paste and spread it inside the circles.
5. Core the pears or halve and pit the peaches. Slice the fruit thinly and mix with the demerara sugar, cinnamon, and finely chopped rosemary.
6. Arrange the fruit on top of the almond paste in shape of a fan and sprinkle slivered almonds on top.
7. Put thin slices of cold butter on top and bake the flans in the center of the oven for 20–25 minutes or until golden.
8. Dust the flans with confectioner's sugar.

# strawberry flan with toffee cream

These wonderful flans are perfect to make in the summertime. Plenty of pleasure for almost no work.

MAKES 2 FLANS/SERVES 10

9 oz fresh puff pastry

egg for brushing

4 oz good-quality dark chocolate (70% cocoa solids)

2 batches of butterscotch cream, see recipe page 211

4 1/2 cups fresh strawberries, hulled and sliced

1. Preheat the oven to 350°F.
2. Roll out pastry to a rectangle and cut four strips, each 1/2 in wide from a long edge. Divide the remaining pastry in half.
3. Line a baking sheet with wax paper. Transfer the two pieces of pastry to the baking sheet and brush the edges with beaten egg. Stick the pastry strips to the long edges.
4. Brush the pastry with egg, prick the center of the flans with a fork, and bake in the center of the oven for about 25 minutes.
5. Meanwhile, chop the chocolate coarsely and melt it in a bowl set over a pan of simmering water.
6. Brush the freshly baked flans with melted chocolate within the edges.
7. When the chocolate has set, spoon butterscotch cream onto the flans and arrange sliced strawberries on top.

# raspberry lemon meringue pie

I top my version of the classic lemon meringue pie with raspberry meringue. The sourness from the lemon and the sweetness of the meringue are perfects partners. When you are making meringue, be careful not to let any of the egg yolk slip into the bowl with the whites. Fat from the yolk will prevent the formation of good foam, and you will end up without any meringue.

MAKES 1 PIE/SERVES 12

1 batch of classic shortcrust pastry
   dough, see recipe page 55
3 batches of lemon curd, see recipe
   page 208
egg for brushing
fresh raspberries for decoration
confectioner's sugar

RASPBERRY MERINGUE

3 organic egg whites
juice of 1/2 lemon
1 1/3 cups sugar
3/4 cup fresh raspberries

1. Prepare the dough according to the basic recipe.
2. Roll out the pastry on a lighlty floured surface and line a loose-bottomed pie tin. Transfer to the freezer.
3. Preheat the oven to 350°F.
4. Brush the bottom of the frozen crust with beaten egg and prick the bottom of the crust with a fork, then prebake for about 10 minutes until lightly golden.
5. Fill the pastry case with foil or beans.
6. When the pie case is cool, fill it with lemon curd.
7. Increase the oven temperature to 475°F.
8. In a stainless steel bowl, beat together the egg whites, lemon juice, and 2/3 cup sugar to stiff peaks.
9. Fold in another 2/3 cup sugar.
10. Mix the raspberries with the remaining sugar until the raspberries separate. Carefully blend the raspberries in batches into the meringue. Beat the meringue until firmly peaking.
11. Pipe or spread the meringue on top of the pie and bake in the center of the oven with the oven door ajar for about 5 minutes or until the meringue starts to turn golden.
12. Decorate the pie with fresh raspberries and dust the top with confectioner's sugar.

# cupcakes & muffins

The first thing I ever learned to bake was a classic muffin under the supervision of my granny. There are dozens of muffin recipes, and I have collected together my own favorites in this chapter. The cupcake, or fairy cake, is a close and popular cousin to the muffin. The main difference is that cupcakes have icing on top.

# classic cupcakes

Cupcakes are a fun alternative to a traditional cake when you are having a party. These sweet little jewels are great with either cream cheese or white chocolate frosting—choose whichever you prefer! I always put the paper liners in a muffin tin because it makes the cupcakes rise to splendid heights.

MAKES 12 CAKES

BASIC RECIPE

3 organic eggs

1 cup sugar

1 teaspoon vanilla sugar

$1/2$ cup unsalted butter

$1/3$ cup milk

2 cups all-purpose flour

2 teaspoons baking powder

1 pinch of salt

zest and juice of 1 lemon

sprinkles or crystallized flowers for decoration

CREAM CHEESE FROSTING

$1/4$ cup plus 1 tablespoon unsalted butter, softened

2 $1/2$ cups confectioner's sugar

1 teaspoon vanilla sugar

1 tablespoon freshly squeezed lemon juice

4 oz cream cheese

a few drops of food coloring

WHITE CHOCOLATE FROSTING

7 oz good-quality white chocolate

7 oz cream cheese

1. Preheat the oven to 350°F.
2. Beat together the eggs, butter, and vanilla sugar until pale and fluffy.
3. Melt the butter, pour in the milk, and blend with the egg mixture.
4. Mix together the flour, baking powder, and salt and carefully fold into the mixture.
5. Add the lemon zest and juice to the mixture.
6. Put paper liners in a muffin tin and pour in the mixture until the liners are two-thirds full.
7. Bake in the center of the oven for about 15 minutes. Leave to cool.
8. Make the cream cheese frosting by mixing together the butter, confectioner's sugar, vanilla sugar, lemon juice, and cream cheese until creamy.
9. If you want frosting in a few different colors, divide the frosting into separate bowls and mix in the chosen food color or leave it white.
10. Spread the frosting over the cupcakes and decorate with sprinkles or flowers.
11. Alternatively, make white chocolate frosting. Chop the chocolate and melt in a bowl set it over a pan of simmering water. Leave to cool a little.
12. Mix the chocolate with cream cheese and spread it over the cakes.

# chocolate cupcakes

MAKES 12 CAKES

BASIC RECIPE

3 organic eggs

1 cup sugar

1 teaspoon vanilla sugar

¼ cup unsalted butter

½ cup sour cream

2 tablespoons cold coffee

2 cups all-purpose flour

2 teaspoons baking powder

5 tablespoons good-quality cocoa powder

1 pinch of salt

4 oz good-quality dark chocolate (70% cocoa solids)

sprinkles or crystallized flowers for decoration

CHOCOLATE FROSTING

¼ cup plus 1 tablespoon unsalted butter, softened

2 ½ cups confectioner's sugar

1 teaspoon vanilla sugar

¼ cup good-quality cocoa powder

4 oz cream cheese

1 tablespoon warm coffee

1. Preheat the oven to 350°F.

2. Beat together the eggs, butter, and vanilla sugar until pale and fluffy.

3. Melt the butter, add the sour cream and coffee and blend with the egg mixture.

4. Mix together the flour, baking powder, cocoa powder and salt and carefully fold into the mixture.

5. Chop the chocolate coarsely and melt it in a bowl set over a pan of simmering water. Add to the mixture.

6. Put paper liners in a muffin tin and pour in the mixture until the liners are two-thirds full.

7. Bake in the center of the oven for about 15 minutes. Leave to cool.

8. Make the frosting by mixing together the butter, confectioner's sugar, vanilla sugar, cocoa powder, and cream cheese until creamy. Stir in the coffee.

9. Spread the frosting over the cupcakes and decorate with sprinkles or flowers.

# raspberry cupcakes

MAKES 12 CAKES

1 batch of classic cupcake mixture, see recipe page 85

½ cup fresh or frozen raspberries

RASPBERRY FROSTING

1 ¼ cups confectioner's sugar

5 oz cream cheese

½ cup fresh or frozen raspberries, and extra for decoration

1. Prepare the mixture according to the basic recipe and carefully blend in the raspberries.

2. Put paper liners in a muffin tin and pour in the mixture until the liners are two-thirds full.

3. Bake in the center of the preheated oven for about 15 minutes. Leave to cool.

4. Make the frosting by mixing together the confectioner's sugar and cream cheese until creamy.

5. Carefully blend in the raspberries and spread the frosting over the cupcakes.

6. Decorate with fresh raspberries.

# lemon poppy seed cupcakes

A cupcake mixture is traditionally a bit denser than a muffin mixture. I mix the mixture thoroughly until it's smooth before filling the paper liners. Lemon and poppy seeds are a brilliant mix, and I discovered this delightful yet sour innovation when I lived in New York. They soon became my favorites, and I never get tired of these wonderful, fresh cupcakes. Try them and you won't be disappointed!

**MAKES 12 CAKES**

1 batch of classic cupcake mixture,
  see recipe page 85
1/2 cup poppy seeds
zest of 2 lemons
juice of 1 lemon
poppy seeds and white currants for
  decoration

**LEMON CREAM CHEESE FROSTING**

1/4 cup plus 1 tablespoon soft butter
2 1/2 cups confectioner's sugar
1 teaspoon vanilla sugar
zest of 2 lemons
juice of 1/2 lemon
4 oz cream cheese

1. Prepare the mixture according to the basic recipe. Add the poppy seeds and the additional lemon zest and lemon juice.
2. Put paper liners in a muffin tin and pour in the mixture until the liners are two-thirds full.
3. Bake in the center of the preheated oven for about 15 minutes. Leave to cool.
4. Make the frosting by mixing together the butter, confectioner's sugar, vanilla sugar, lemon zest, lemon juice, and cream cheese until creamy.
5. Spread the frosting over the cupcakes and decorate with poppy seeds and white currants.

# banana fudge cupcakes

**MAKES 12 CAKES**

1 batch of chocolate cupcake mixture,
    see recipe page 86
2 bananas, sliced
1 tablespoon ground cinnamon
colored sweets for decoration

**CHOCOLATE FUDGE ICING**

½ cup heavy whipping cream
3 tablespoons honey
5 tablespoons brown sugar
1 teaspoon ground ginger
1 tablespoon unsalted butter
7 oz good-quality dark chocolate (70%
    cocoa solids)

1. Prepare the mixture according to the basic recipe and add the
   sliced bananas and cinnamon.
2. Put paper liners in a muffin tin and pour in the mixture
   until the liners are two-thirds full.
3. Bake in the center of the preheated oven for about 15 minutes.
   Leave to cool.
4. Make the icing by bringing the heavy whipping cream, honey,
   brown sugar, and ginger to a boil. Leave to cool a little.
5. Add the butter and finely chopped chocolate and stir until it
   melts.
6. Leave the mixture to cool slightly before icing the cupcakes.
7. Decorate with sweets.

# blueberry corn muffins

These substantial corn and blueberry muffins are wonderful to eat warm and freshly baked with some butter and flaked salt on top—yummy!

MAKES 12 CAKES

1/2 cup unsalted butter
2 organic eggs
1/2 cup buttermilk
1 3/4 cups all-purpose flour
1 cup cornmeal
2/3 cup sugar
1 teaspoon baking powder
1 pinch of salt
1 tablespoon all-purpose flour for the blueberries
2/3 cup fresh or frozen blueberries
demerara sugar

1. Preheat the oven to 425°F.
2. Melt the butter and beat it with eggs and buttermilk.
3. Mix the flour, cornmeal, sugar, baking powder, and salt in a bowl.
4. Pour the dry ingredients into the egg mixture and fold in carefully. Don't worry if there are small lumps of flour in the mixture.
5. Toss the blueberries in the flour and carefully fold into the mixture.
6. Put paper liners in a muffin tin and pour in the mixture until the liners are two-thirds full.
7. Sprinkle demerara sugar on top of each muffin and bake in the center of the oven for about 20 minutes or until a skewer inserted into the center comes out clean.

# peanut butter cupcakes

There are loads of delicious frostings you can use to ice your cupcakes, and there are no limits to how you decorate them. This frosting is as tasty as it is simple to make.

MAKES 12 CAKES

1 batch of chocolate cupcake mixture, see recipe page 86
1 cup salted peanuts and extra for decoration

PEANUT BUTTER FROSTING

1/2 cup smooth peanut butter
2 cups confectioner's sugar
5 tablespoons good-quality cocoa powder
2 teaspoons vanilla sugar
5 oz cream cheese
1 tablespoon warm coffee

1. Prepare the mixture according to the basic recipe.
2. Put paper liners in a muffin tin.
3. Chop the peanuts and add them to the paper liners, layering them with the cake batter until two-thirds full.
4. Bake in the center of the preheated oven for about 15 minutes. Leave to cool.
5. Stir the peanut butter, confectioner's sugar, cocoa powder, vanilla sugar, and cream cheese until creamy. Stir in the coffee.
6. Spread the frosting on top of the cakes and decorate with extra peanuts.

# carrot, ginger, walnut cupcakes

When it comes to carrot cupcakes, the key to success is to put lots of flavor into the mixture. I like ginger, but you can vary the flavoring and use ground cloves or allspice instead.

MAKES 12 CAKES

3 organic eggs

1 ¼ cups sugar

1 ¾ cups all-purpose flour

1 teaspoon vanilla sugar

1 tablespoon baking powder

1 pinch of salt

1 ½ teaspoons ground cinnamon

1 teaspoon ground cardamom

2 teaspoons ground ginger

½ cup sunflower oil

4 cups grated carrots

½ cup walnuts chopped

whole walnuts for decoration

CREAM CHEESE LIME FROSTING

¼ cup plus 1 tablespoon soft butter

2 ½ cups confectioner's sugar

1 teaspoon vanilla sugar

zest of 1 lime

4 oz cream cheese

1. Preheat the oven to 350°F.
2. Beat the eggs and the sugar until pale and fluffy.
3. Mix together the dry ingredients and fold into the egg mixture.
4. Stir in the oil, carrots, and coarsely chopped walnuts.
5. Put paper liners in a muffin tin and pour in the mixture until the liners are two-thirds full.
6. Bake in the center of the oven for 12–15 minutes. Leave to cool.
7. Make the frosting by mixing together the ingredients until creamy.
8. Spread the frosting on top of the cupcakes and decorate each one with a whole walnut.

# high-hat cupcakes

These fantastic-looking cupcakes should be served cold. You can keep them in the refrigerator for about three days, but cover them carefully in pastic wrap to keep them fresh. They are the yummiest of cupcakes.

MAKES 12 CAKES
1 batch of chocolate cupcake mixture,
    see recipe page 86

MERINGUE TOPPING
6 organic egg whites
3 ½ cups sugar
juice of 1 lemon
2 teaspoons vanilla sugar

CHOCOLATE COATING
12 oz good-quality dark chocolate (70%
    cocoa solids)
4 tablespoons vegetable oil

1. Prepare the cupcakes according to the basic recipe. Bake them in the preheated oven for 15 minutes. Leave to cool.
2. In a stainless steel bowl, mix together the egg whites, sugar, and lemon juice. Beat by hand for about 1 minute until fluffy.
3. Rest the bowl over a pan of boiling water. Beat until the sugar crystals have dissolved and the mixture has a consistency as fluffy as meringue. You should see the trail from the whisk in the foam.
4. Remove the bowl from the pan and beat the vanilla sugar into the foam. Use a hand-held electric beater to mix the meringue for a few minutes until it is thick and cool.
5. Put the meringue in a piping bag with a round nozzle and pipe the meringue on top of the cupcakes spirals. Leave about a half-inch around the edges.
6. Leave to set in the refrigerator.
7. Make the coating. Chop the chocolate and melt it with vegetable oil in a bowl set over a pan of simmering water.
8. Pour the chocolate into a small bowl and leave to cool.
9. Take the cupcakes out of the fridge and dip each peak in the chocolate. Brush on additional chocolate if there are any gaps.
10. Leave to set on a plate in the refrigerator for about 30 minutes.

# nine classic muffins

When I'm baking muffins, I mix the dry ingredients and the liquids separately. Then I blend everything together quickly, without stirring too much. Don't worry if there are small lumps of flour in the mixture; the muffins will still turn out gorgeously fluffy and amazingly moist.

MAKES 6 LARGE/12 SMALL
   MUFFINS
BASIC RECIPE
½ cup unsalted butter
¾ cup milk
zest of 1 lemon
2 organic eggs
⅔ cup sugar
1 teaspoon vanilla sugar
2 ⅓ cups all-purpose flour
2 teaspoons baking powder
1 pinch of salt

1. Preheat the oven to 350°F for large muffins and 400°F if you want to make small muffins.
2. Melt the butter and add the milk and lemon zest.
3. Beat together the eggs, sugar, and vanilla sugar until pale and fluffy.
4. Stir the butter mixture into the egg mixture.
5. Mix together the flour, baking powder, and salt and carefully fold into the mixture.
6. Put paper liners in a muffin tin and pour in the mixture until the liners are two-thirds full.
7. Bake in the center of the oven for about 20 minutes for large muffins or 12–15 minutes for small ones. A skewer inserted into the center should come out clean.

## malteser muffins

MAKES 6 LARGE/12 SMALL
   MUFFINS
1 batch of muffin mixture, see basic recipe above and instructions
¼ cup unsalted butter (extra)
2 oz good-quality cocoa powder (instead of ⅓ cup flour)
¾ cup sour cream (instead of milk)
1 bag of chocolate-coated malted milk balls

1. Prepare the muffin mixture according to the basic recipe but add ¼ cup extra butter, replace ⅓ cup of the flour with cocoa powder, and use sour cream instead of the milk.
2. Put paper liners in a muffin tin and pour in the mixture until the liners are two-thirds full.
3. Stick a few chocolate-coated malt balls in every muffin and bake in the center of the preheated oven for about 20 minutes for large muffins or 12–15 minutes for small ones.

## forest berry muffins

MAKES 6 LARGE/12 SMALL
   MUFFINS
1 batch of muffin mixture, see basic recipe above
1 ¼ cups fresh or frozen blueberries, blackberries, and raspberries

1. Prepare the muffin mixture according to the basic recipe.
2. Put paper liners in a muffin tin. Layer the berries with the muffin batter until the paper liners are two-thirds full.
3. Bake in the center of the preheated oven for about 20 minutes for large muffins or 12–15 minutes for small ones.

# cherry muffins

MAKES 6 LARGE/12 SMALL
    MUFFINS
1 batch of muffin mixture, see basic
    recipe page 98
1 1/2 cups fresh cherries

1. Prepare the muffin mixture according to the basic recipe.
2. Wash and pit cherries.
3. Put paper liners in a muffin tin. Layer the cherries and muffin batter in the paper liners until they are two-thirds full.
4. Bake in the center of the preheated oven for about 20 minutes for large muffins or 12–15 minutes for small ones.

# orange chocolate muffins

MAKES 6 LARGE/12 SMALL
    MUFFINS
1 batch of muffin mixture, see basic
    recipe page 98
zest of 2 oranges
7 oz orange-flavored chocolate

1. Prepare the muffin mixture according to the basic recipe and add the orange zest.
2. Put paper liners in a muffin tin and carefully pour in the mixture until the liners are two-thirds full.
3. Add a few pieces of chocolate to each muffin.
4. Bake in the center of the preheated oven for about 20 minutes for large muffins or 12–15 minutes for small ones.

# banana chocolate chip muffins

MAKES 6 LARGE/12 SMALL
    MUFFINS
1 batch of muffin mixture, see basic
    recipe page 98 and instructions
1/4 cup unsalted butter (extra)
1/2 cup good-quality cocoa powder
    (instead of 1/3 cup flour)
1 cup sour cream (instead of milk)
3 ripe bananas
7 oz good quality dark chocolate (70%
    cocoa solids)

1. Prepare the muffin mixture according to the basic recipe but add extra butter and cocoa powder (instead of 1/3 cup flour), and replace the milk with sour cream.
2. Put paper liners in a muffin tin.
3. Slice the bananas and chop the chocolate coarsely. Reserving some of the chocolate pieces for decoration, layer the banana, chocolate, and muffin batter in the paper liners until they are two-thirds full.
4. Bake in the center of the preheated oven for about 20 minutes for large muffins or 12–15 minutes for small ones.

# snickers muffins

MAKES 6 LARGE/12 SMALL
    MUFFINS
1 batch of muffin mixture, see basic
    recipe page 98
1 bag of mini Snickers

1. Prepare the muffin mixture according to the basic recipe.
2. Put paper liners in a muffin tin and carefully pour in the mixture until the liners are two-thirds full.
3. Stick a few mini Snickers in each muffin and bake in the center of the preheated oven for about 20 minutes for large muffins or 12–15 minutes for small ones.

# pineapple muffins with coconut & lime

MAKES 6 LARGE/12 SMALL
MUFFINS

1 batch of muffin mixture, see basic
recipe page 98

1/2 fresh or canned pineapple

1/4 cup unsweetened coconut

zest of 3 limes

1. Prepare the muffin mixture according to the basic recipe.
2. Remove the skin and core from the pineapple and cut the flesh in pieces. If you use canned pineapple, cut the rings in pieces.
3. Toast the unsweetened coconut in a dry saucepan, reserving half for decoration.
4. Add the pineapple, roasted unsweetened coconut, and lime zest to the mixture and stir to combine.
5. Put paper liners in a muffin tin and carefully pour in the mixture until the liners are two-thirds full. Sprinkle each muffin with the reserved unsweetened coconut.
6. Bake in the center of the preheated oven for about 20 minutes for large muffins or 12–15 minutes for small ones.

# cinnamon & ginger muffins

MAKES 6 LARGE/12 SMALL
MUFFINS

1 batch of muffin mixture, see basic
recipe page 98

2 teaspoons ground cinnamon

1 teaspoon ground ginger

2 teaspoons ground clove

2 handfuls of slivered almonds

2 teaspoons orange zest

1. Prepare the muffin mixture according to the basic muffin recipe but bring the spices to a boil with milk. Leave the milk to cool before you blend it in the mixture.
2. Toast two-thirds of the slivered almonds in a dry saucepan.
3. Blend slivered almonds and orange zest the mixture.
4. Place paper liners in a muffin tin and carefully pour in the mixture until the liners are two-thirds full.
5. Sprinkle the unroasted slivered almonds on top of the muffins.
6. Bake in the center of the preheated oven for about 20 minutes for large muffins or 12–15 minutes for small ones.

# wild strawberry & cardamom muffins

MAKES 6 LARGE/12 SMALL
MUFFINS

2 tablespoons cardamom pods

1 batch of muffin mixture, see basic
recipe page 98

1/3 cup fresh wild strawberries

1 handful of slivered almonds

1. Pound the cardamom pods in a mortar. Put the milk in a saucepan, add the cardamom, and bring to a boil. Leave to infuse. When the milk is cool, prepare the mixture according to the basic muffin recipe.
2. Put paper liners in a muffin tin. Layer the strawberries with the muffin batter until the liners are two-thirds full.
3. Sprinkle slivered almonds on top of the muffins.
4. Bake in the center of the preheated oven for about 20 minutes for large muffins or 12–15 minutes for small ones.

# blueberry muffins with crumble

These are definitely my favorite muffins. They are like an unbelievably juicy combination of muffins and crumble.

MAKES 6 LARGE MUFFINS

1 batch of muffin mixture, see basic recipe page 98

2 1/4 cups fresh or frozen blueberries

CRUMBLE

1/4 cup plus 2 tablespoons cold, unsalted butter

1 cup rolled oats

1/2 cup plus 1 tablespoon all-purpose flour

1/4 cup plus 3 tablespoons sugar

1. Preheat the oven to 350ºF.
2. Prepare the muffin mixture according to the basic muffin recipe.
3. Put paper liners in a muffin tin. Reserving some of the blueberries for decoration, layer the berries and muffin battter in the paper liners until they are two-thirds full.
4. Make the crumble. Dice the butter and put it in a bowl with the oats, flour, and sugar. Mix it with your fingertips to make breadcrumbs.
5. Sprinkle some of the crumble on top of each muffin and decorate with reserved blueberries.
6. Bake for about 20 minutes in the center of the oven.

# apple cinnamon muffins with crumble

MAKES 6 LARGE MUFFINS

1 batch of muffin mixture, see basic recipe page 98

4 large apples

3 tablespoons butter

3 tablespoons sugar

1 tablespoon cinnamon

CRUMBLE

1/4 cup plus 2 tablespoons cold, unsalted butter

1 cup rolled oats

1/2 cup plus 1 tablespoon all-purpose flour

1/4 cup plus 3 tablespoons sugar

1. Preheat the oven to 350ºF.
2. Prepare the muffin mixture according to the basic muffin recipe.
3. Remove the cores from the apples and cut into slices. Fry the apples with the butter, sugar, and cinnamon in a hot pan for a few minutes. Leave to cool.
4. Put paper liners in a muffin tin. Reserving six apple slices for decoration, mix the remainder with the muffin batter and fill the paper liners to two-thirds full.
5. Make the crumble. Dice the butter and put it in a bowl with the oats, flour, and sugar. Mix it with your fingertips to make breadcrumbs.
6. Sprinkle some crumble on top of each muffin and decorate with a slice of apple.
7. Bake for about 20 minutes in the center of the oven.

# brownie cupcakes

MAKES 16 MUFFINS
2 organic eggs
¾ cup sugar
1 teaspoon vanilla sugar
¼ cup butter
¼ cup cooking oil
¼ cup plus 2 tablespoons golden syrup
   or light corn syrup
1 ¼ cups all-purpose flour
⅓ cup good-quality cocoa powder
1 teaspoon baking powder
1 pinch of salt
4 oz good-quality dark chocolate (70%
   cocoa solids)
Heavy whipping cream and fresh berries
   for decoration

1. Preheat the oven to 350°F.
2. Beat together the eggs, sugar, and vanilla sugar until pale and fluffy.
3. Melt the butter and mix it with cooking oil and syrup. Stir into the egg mixture.
4. Mix together the flour, cocoa powder, baking powder, and salt and carefully fold into the mixture.
5. Chop the chocolate and melt it in a bowl set over a pan of simmering water. Blend it into the mixture.
6. Put paper liners in a muffin tin and carefully pour in the mixture until the liners are two-thirds full.
7. Bake for about 12 minutes in the center of the oven. The muffins will fall flat in the center when removed from the oven.
8. Decorate with lightly whipped cream and fresh berries.

# spanish meringue

I got the idea to color meringues from a patisserie in Barcelona. They had meringues in lots of fun pastel colors. You can vary these classic meringues with different flavorings. For example, it's delicious to mix in roasted slivered almonds in the meringues.

MAKES 9 MERINGUES

7 organic egg whites
2 ½ cups sugar
juice of 1 lemon
4 oz good-quality dark chocolate (70% cocoa solids) or red food coloring

1. Preheat the oven to 250°F.
2. Mix together the egg whites, sugar, and lemon juice in a stainless steel bowl.
3. Place the bowl over a pan of simmering water. Beat by hand until the sugar crystals have dissolved and the meringue is 140–155°F.
4. Take the bowl from the pan and beat the meringue with a hand-held electric mixer until the meringue is thick and has cooled.
5. For chocolatey meringues, melt the chopped chocolate in a bowl set over a pan of simmering water and carefully blend it into the meringue to make it striped. To make pink meringues, beat about 10 drops of red food coloring into the meringue and blend until it is an even pink color.
6. Use two teaspoons to drop the mixture into paper liners or onto a baking sheet covered with parchment paper.
7. Bake in the center of the oven for about 1 hour. The meringues should be a bit chewy in the center when they are cooked.

# party cakes

Nothing makes a party more than a cake. My favorites are those with berries, although I also love the Swedish classics Almond Tosca and Princess Cake. Ideally, a cake should be quick and easy to make, but some of these recipes do require a little more time and patience because they have to be made in stages. One tip is to read through the whole recipe carefully before you start. This will give you a sense of the timing and will prepare you for the task ahead.

It is easier to construct this cake if you push a skewer through the two lower tiers to hold them together. Allow the meringue cream and chocolate mousse to set a little by cooling them in the fridge for a while before you assemble the cake because this will make them easier to spread.

# my most romantic wedding cake

Making a wedding cake is never easy, and it's probably not a task for the stressed-out and nervous wife or husband-to-be. But if you have a relative who enjoys baking, this beautiful wedding cake is quite simple to make.

MAKES 1 CAKE/SERVES 26

LEMON SPONGE

6 organic eggs

2 cups sugar

2 teaspoons vanilla sugar

1/2 cup unsalted butter and extra for greasing the cake pans

3/4 cup plus 2 tablespoons milk

4 cups all-purpose flour

1 tablespoon baking powder

zest and juice of 2 lemons

CHOCOLATE SPONGE

3 organic eggs

1 cup sugar

1 teaspoon vanilla sugar

1/4 cup butter

1/4 cup plus 3 tablespoons sour cream

2 cups plus 2 tablespoons all-purpose flour

2 teaspoons baking powder

5 tablespoons good-quality cocoa powder

4 oz good-quality dark chocolate (70% cocoa solids)

3 tablespoons cold coffee

WHITE CHOCOLATE MOUSSE

5 oz good-quality white chocolate

3/4 cup plus 2 tablespoons heavy whipping cream

1 cup cottage cheese

zest of 1 lemon

1. Preheat the oven to 350°F.
2. Make the lemon sponge. Beat together the eggs, sugar, and vanilla sugar until pale and fluffy.
3. Melt the butter and stir in the milk. Add to the egg mixture.
4. Mix together the flour and baking powder and carefully fold into the mixture. Stir in the lemon zest and juice.
5. Butter one 10 in and three 6 in nonstick cake pans.
6. Pour half of the mixture into the big pan and distribute the rest into the small pans. Bake in the center of the oven for 15–20 minutes or until a skewer inserted into the center comes out clean.
7. Make the chocolate sponge. Beat together the eggs, sugar, and vanilla sugar until pale and fluffy.
8. Melt the butter and stir in the sour cream. Add to the egg mixture.
9. Mix together the flour, baking powder, and cocoa powder and carefully fold into the mixture.
10. Melt the chocolate in a bowl set over a pan of simmering water. Stir the chocolate and the coffee into the mixture.
11. Butter one 10 in and one 6 in nonstick cake pan.
12. Pour two-thirds of the mixture into the larger pan and the rest into the small pan.
13. Bake in the center of the preheated oven for 15–20 minutes or until a skewer inserted into the center comes out clean.
14. Make the white chocolate mousse. Chop the chocolate and melt it in a bowl set over a pan of simmering water.
15. Whip the cream. Blend the cottage cheese and the lemon zest into the cream.
16. Blend the cream and cottage cheese mixture into the chocolate a little at a time and stir until the mousse is smooth.

*(continued on next page)*

party cakes

111

## DARK CHOCOLATE MOUSSE

4 oz good quality dark chocolate (70% cocoa solids)

1 organic egg yolk

1 tablespoon dark muscovado sugar

½ teaspoon warm coffee

1 tablespoon dark rum

zest and juice of 1 orange

½ cup heavy whipping cream

## WHITE MERINGUE CREAM

4 organic egg whites

1 cup plus 3 tablespoons sugar

juice of 1 lemon

1 ½ cups unsalted butter, softened

## ASSEMBLING

1 batch of syrup, see recipe page 210

4 tablespoons dark rum

1 ¼ cups fresh raspberries

1 cup white currants (or blueberries)

17. Make the dark chocolate mousse. Chop the chocolate coarsely and melt it in a bowl set over a pan of simmering water.

18. Beat together the egg yolk and the sugar until creamy. Stir in the coffee, rum, orange zest, and juice.

19. Mix the warm, melted chocolate into the egg mixture. Whip the cream lightly (it should be thickening but still runny) and blend it a little at a time into the chocolate mixture.

20. Leave the mousse to set slightly in the refrigerator.

21. Make the meringue cream. Mix together the egg whites, sugar, and lemon juice in a stainless steel bowl.

22. Place the bowl over a pan of boiling water. Beat until the mixture thickens, the sugar crystals have dissolved, and the meringue is 140–155°F.

23. Remove the bowl from the heat and beat the meringue with a hand-held electric mixer, gradually adding the butter, until it is smooth and cool.

24. Leave the meringue to set in the refrigerator.

25. Cut the large lemon sponge in half horizontally. Trim the top of the large chocolate sponge to make it level.

26. Place one of the lemon sponge layers on a cake stand. Mix the syrup with the rum and brush the surface of the cake with the mixture.

27. Fill a piping bag with meringue and pipe a circle of meringue around the edge. Fill the center with white chocolate mousse.

28. Put the large chocolate cake on top and brush with the syrup and rum.

29. Pipe a circle of meringue around the edge. Fill the center with dark chocolate mousse and press some fresh raspberries into the mousse.

30. Put the second large lemon layer on top and cover it with a thin layer of meringue.

31. Trim two of the small lemon sponges to make two layers, each about three-fourths in thick. Trim the small chocolate cake in the same way.

32. Layer the small lemon and chocolate cakes together, repeating steps 26-30.

33. From the last lemon sponge, cut out two small cakes with a glass or a biscuit cutter.

34. Put one of the small cakes on top of the cake and pipe a circle of meringue around the edge. Fill the center with dark chocolate mousse and raspberries. Put the other small cake on top.

35. Cover the whole cake with a thin layer of meringue and arrange currants around each tier.

# redberry trifle

Trifle is extremely easy to make, and it makes an impressive and colorful centerpiece at any birthday party. If you want to take a shortcut, you can use ready-made sponge.

SERVES 16

1 batch of sponge mixture, see basic
   recipe page 30
1 ³/₄ cups heavy whipping cream
2 cups plus 2 tablespoons low-fat Greek
   yogurt
4 oz homemade almond paste, see recipe
   page 208
¼ cup plus 3 tablespoons Marsala
⅓ cup light muscovado sugar
4 ½ cups fresh strawberries
4 cups fresh raspberries and redcurrants
   or blueberries

1. Bake the sponge according to the basic recipe. Use a rectangular cake pan, buttered and covered with breadcrumbs. Leave to cool.
2. Cut the sponge into three-fourth in slices.
3. Whip the cream and mix it first with the yogurt and then with grated almond paste.
4. Bring the Marsala and the muscovado sugar to the boil. Leave to cool a little.
5. Slice the strawberries and put them together with the berries in the just-warm wine.
6. Arrange the cake, fruit, and cream in layers in a glass bowl, starting with cake, then fruit, then cream. Finish with a layer of fruit.

# mom's swiss roll

This is the simplest and quickest cake in the world; it takes only 5 minutes in the oven. Roll up the cake when it's warm if you are filling it with jam or berries. If you are using hazelnut and chocolate spread or cream for the filling, you should leave it to cool under a tea towel before rolling it; otherwise the filling will melt.

MAKES 1 CAKE

BASIC RECIPE

3 organic eggs

½ cup plus 2 tablespoons sugar

3 tablespoons milk

zest of 1 orange

1 cup plus 3 tablespoons all-purpose flour

1 teaspoon baking powder

1 handful slivered almonds

caster sugar for rolling

1. Preheat the oven to 450°F.
2. Beat together the eggs and the sugar until pale and fluffy.
3. Add the milk and the orange zest.
4. Mix the flour with the baking powder and fold into the egg mixture.
5. Spread the mixture thinly and evenly in a Swiss roll pan lined with parchment paper.
6. Sprinkle the slivered almonds on top and bake in the center of the oven for about 5 minutes.
7. Sprinkle sugar on a piece of parchment paper and turn out the cake upside down.
8. Carefully loosen the parchment paper from the cake base.
9. Fill the cake with a filling of your choice. See variations below and on pages 118-9.

## summer cloudberry swiss roll

MAKES 1 CAKE

1 batch of Mom's Swiss Roll, see basic recipe above

3 ½ tablespoons sugar

4 cups fresh or frozen cloudberries or raspberries

¼ cup cloudberry or raspberry jam

1. Prepare and cook the cake according to the basic recipe.
2. Mix together the sugar and the cloudberries and drain away excess liquid.
3. Mix the berries with the jam and spread the filling over the cake in an even layer.
4. Roll the cake from one long side toward the other, making sure you tuck in the first long side tightly.
5. Cut the cake into half-inch thick slices.

## forest berry swiss roll

MAKES 1 CAKE

1 batch of Mom's Swiss Roll, see basic recipe above

3 ¾ cups mixed fresh or frozen blueberries, blackberries, and raspberries

¼ cup plus 2 tablespoons muscovado sugar

1. Prepare and cook the cake according to the basic recipe.
2. Mix together the muscovado sugar and the berries and drain away excess liquid.
3. Spread the fruit evenly over the cake.
4. Roll the cake from one long side toward the other, making sure you tuck in the first long side tightly.
5. Cut the cake into half-inch thick slices.

party cakes

## almond and amaretto swiss roll

MAKES 1 CAKE

1 batch of Mom's Swiss Roll, see basic
    recipe on page 117

1/4 cup Amaretto liquor

1 batch of syrup, see recipe on page 210

3/4 cup plus 2 tablespoons heavy
    whipping cream

1/4 cup plus 3 tablespoons low-fat Greek
    yogurt

5 oz homemade almond paste, see
    recipe page 208

1. Prepare and cook the cake according to the basic recipe.
2. Mix the Amaretto with the syrup and brush the mixture over the freshly baked cake.
3. Whip the cream and mix it first with the yogurt and then with grated almond paste.
4. Spread the filling over the cake in an even layer.
5. Roll the cake from one long side toward the other, making sure you tuck in the first long side tightly.
6. Cut the cake into half-inch thick slices.

## chocolate & banana swiss roll

MAKES 1 CAKE

1 batch of Mom's Swiss Roll, see basic
    recipe on page 117

1/4 cup butter, melted

3 1/2 tablespoons good-quality cocoa
    powder (instead of 3 1/2 tablespoons
    all-purpose flour)

3/4 jar of hazelnut and chocolate spread

2 ripe bananas

1. Prepare the cake according to the basic recipe but add melted butter and replace 1/4 cup of the flour with cocoa powder.
2. Bake the cake for about 4 minutes and turn it out according to the basic recipe. Leave to cool a little.
3. Spread chocolate spread over the freshly baked cake and sprinkle over the thinly sliced bananas.
4. Roll the cake from one long side toward the other, making sure you tuck in the first long side tightly.
5. Cut the cake into half-inch thick slices.

## blueberry & lemon swiss roll

MAKES 1 CAKE

1 batch of Mom's Swiss Roll, see basic
    recipe page 117

zest of 2 lemons

5 cups fresh or frozen blueberries

1/4 cup plus 3 tablespoons sugar

1. Prepare and cook the cake according to the basic recipe, but use lemon zest instead of the orange zest.
2. Mix together the sugar and the blueberries and drain away the excess liquid.
3. Spread the fruit over the cake.
4. Roll the cake from one long side toward the other, making sure you tuck in the first long side tightly.
5. Cut the cake into half-inch thick slices.

# cardamom swiss roll with red berries

MAKES 1 CAKE

1 batch of Mom's Swiss Roll, see basic
recipe page 117

¾ cup fresh or frozen red currants or
blueberries

2 ¼ cups fresh strawberries

½ teaspoon cardamom pods

3 tablespoons balsamic vinegar

¼ cup demerara sugar

1. Prepare and cook the cake according to the basic recipe.
2. Remove the stalks from the redcurrants and hull and thinly
slice the strawberries.
3. Pound the cardamom in a mortar.
4. Mix together the fruit, cardamom, vinegar, and sugar. Drain
away the excess liquid.
5. Spread the fruit over the cake.
6. Roll the cake from one long side toward the other, making
sure you tuck in the first long side tightly.
7. Cut the cake into half-inch thick slices.

# jam swiss roll

MAKES 1 CAKE

1 batch of Mom's Swiss Roll, see basic
recipe page 117

1 cup raspberry jam

1. Prepare and cook the cake according to the basic recipe.
2. Spread the jam evenly over the cake.
3. Roll the cake from one long side toward the other, making
sure you tuck in the first long side tightly.
4. Cut the cake into half-inch thick slices.

# strawberry & basil swiss roll

MAKES 1 CAKE

1 batch of Mom's Swiss Roll, see basic
recipe page 117

2 ¼ cups fresh strawberries

¼ cup plus 3 tablespoons sugar

1 bunch of fresh basil

zest of 1 lime

1. Prepare and cook the cake according to the basic recipe.
2. Hull and thinly slice the strawberries and mix with the sugar.
Drain away the excess liquid.
3. Mix the chopped basil and lime zest with the strawberries.
Spread the filling evenly over the cake.
4. Roll the cake from one long side toward the other, making
sure you tuck in the first long side tightly.
5. Cut the cake into half-inch thick slices.

# classic light sponge

Use a soft and airy fat-free sponge for patisserie-style cakes like the Princess Cake. You can buy them ready-made but why should you? It's easy to make them yourself, and homemade tastes best!

MAKES 1 CAKE/SERVES 12
BASIC RECIPE
4 organic eggs
½ cup plus 2 tablespoons sugar
¾ cup plus 2 tablespoons all-purpose flour
butter and dried breadcrumbs for the pan

1. Preheat the oven to 400°F.
2. Beat together the eggs and the sugar until pale and fluffy.
3. Fold the flour into the egg mixture.
4. Pour the mixture into a buttered 9 in springform cake pan covered with breadcrumbs.
5. Bake in the center of the oven for 10–15 minutes or until a skewer inserted into the center comes out clean.
6. Leave the sponge to cool slightly in the pan and then turn it out on to a plate or a wire rack.

# princess cake

When I want to give the Princess Cake a slightly more grown-up taste, I mix syrup (see recipe page 210) with Amaretto and brush the mixture over the freshly baked cake layers.

MAKES 1 CAKE/SERVES 12
1 classic cake light sponge, see basic recipe above
1 batch of crème patisserie, see recipe page 209
confectioner's sugar

FILLING
½ cup fresh or frozen raspberries
3 ½ tablespoons sugar
2 ½ cups heavy whipping cream
14 oz pink marzipan (use red or pink food coloring if you can't find pink marzipan)

1. Prepare the cake sponge and the vanilla custard according to the recipes.
2. Cut the cake into three horizontal layers.
3. Use one-third of the crème patisserie to pipe three rounds around the edges of the bottom layer.
4. Mix together the raspberries and sugar and spread the fruit inside the crème patisserie circles.
5. Whip the cream until firm and fluffy. Mix a spoonful of the cream with the crème patisserie and spread some of the mix over the raspberries.
6. Put on the next layer of cake and spread some crème patisserie over the top. Put the last layer in place and spread the remaining crème patisserie on top.
7. Spread the cream over the cake, creating a smooth dome shape.
8. Dust a clean surface with confectioner's sugar and roll out the marzipan.
9. Cover the cake with marzipan, trimming the excess around the edges. Dust the cake with confectioner's sugar.

# strawberry & lemon curd cake

I like to bake some cakes with a regular sponge since it makes the cake really juicy and yummy. You can mix some syrup (see recipe page 210) with your favorite liquor and brush the layers to make them extra delicious.

MAKES 1 CAKE/SERVES 12

1 batch of sponge mixture, see basic recipe page 30

1 batch of lemon curd, see recipe page 208

1 vanilla pod

1/4 cup sugar

4 1/2 cups fresh strawberries

1 cup heavy whipping cream

1. Prepare the sponge mixture according to the basic recipe and pour it into a buttered 9 in springform cake pan covered with breadcrumbs.
2. Bake in the center of the oven for about 25 minutes at 350°F.
3. Leave to cool before cutting it into three horizontal layers.
4. Split the vanilla pod lengthways and scrape out the seeds. Mix the seeds with the sugar. Hull and thinly slice half the strawberries and mix them with the sugar.
5. Put a layer of the cake on a serving plate and cover it with the sliced strawberries.
6. Put another layer of cake on the top and spread over the cool lemon curd.
7. Add the final layer of cake. Beat the cream until it is softly peaking and spread it over the top of the cake. Hull and chop the remaining strawberries and pile them on the cream.

# aunt elsa's party cake

My Aunt Elsa always makes this smashing party cake for my cousin's birthday. It's easy to vary with different fillings and decorations.

MAKES 1 CAKE/SERVES 12

1 batch of sponge mixture, see basic recipe page 30

1/2 batch of crème patisserie, see recipe page 209

1 cup fresh or frozen blueberries

1 cup fresh or frozen strawberries

2 bananas

1/4 cup plus 3 tablespoons sugar

1 cup heavy whipping cream

1. Prepare the sponge mixture according to the basic recipe and pour into a buttered 9 in springform cake pan covered with breadcrumbs.
2. Bake in the center of the oven for about 25 minutes at 350°F.
3. Leave the cake to cool before cutting it into three horizontal layers.
4. Put a layer of the cake on a serving plate and cover it with a layer of cool crème patisserie. Add another layer on top.
5. Mash the berries with the bananas and the sugar. Drain away any excess liquid and spread the fruit over the cake.
6. Put on the top layer of cake and cover the top and sides with lightly whipped cream.

# gluten-free chocolate & hazelnut torte

This is a superb and moist, gluten-free cake, which you also can use as a basic cake sponge if you want to make a gluten-free party cake. Simply spread chocolate and hazelnut spread and sliced bananas on the cake layers and cover the cake with lightly whipped cream and fresh berries.

MAKES 1 CAKE/SERVES 12

2 cups hazelnuts

11 oz good-quality dark chocolate (70% cocoa solids)

1 tablespoon good-quality cocoa powder

¾ cup plus 2 tablespoons unsalted butter, softened

¼ cup plus 3 tablespoons sugar

6 organic eggs, separated

butter for the cake pan

mixed nuts for decoration


PEANUT BUTTER FROSTING

¼ cup soft peanut butter

1 cup plus 3 tablespoons confectioner's sugar

5 tablespoons good-quality cocoa powder

1 teaspoon vanilla sugar

½ cup cream cheese

1 tablespoon warm coffee

1. Preheat the oven to 350°F.
2. Process the hazelnuts in a blender to make a fine powder.
3. Chop 7 oz of the chocolate coarsely and mix it in the blender together with the ground hazelnuts.
4. Add the cocoa powder, butter, and sugar and mix until creamy.
5. Add the egg yolks to the mixture and continue blending.
6. In a clean, dry bowl beat the egg whites until foaming.
7. Carefully blend the whites into the mixture a little at a time.
8. Pour the mixture into a buttered 9 in springform cake pan covered with breadcrumbs. Break the rest of the chocolate into pieces and push them into the mixture.
9. Bake in the center of the oven for 30–35 minutes or until a skewer inserted into the center comes out clean. Remember that the melted pieces of chocolate might make the skewer look sticky even if the cake is ready.
10. Make the frosting. Beat together the peanut butter, confectioner's sugar, cocoa powder, vanilla sugar, and cream cheese until creamy. Add the coffee.
11. Spread the frosting on top of the cake and decorate with mixed nuts.

# chocolate pavlova

Chocolate Pavlova is a delicious cake that is wonderful when decorated with fresh berries in summer. In winter I use fresh dates and clementines and sprinkle pistachio nuts on top. The cake should be assembled just before serving so that the meringue doesn't get soggy. The original cake is named after the prima ballerina Anna Pavlova who was born in Russia at the end of the nineteenth century.

**MAKES 1 CAKE/SERVES 12**

7 organic egg whites
2 ½ cups sugar
juice of 1 lemon
3 tablespoons good-quality cocoa
    powder
³/₄ cup slivered almonds

**TOPPING**

1 ³/₄ cups heavy whipping cream
1 ³/₄ cups low-fat Greek yogurt
3 tablespoons confectioner's sugar
2 ¹/₄ cups fresh berries

1. Preheat the oven to 250°F.
2. Beat together the egg whites, sugar and lemon juice in a stainless steel bowl.
3. Place the bowl over a pan of boiling water and continue beapang until the mixture thickens, sugar crystals have dissolved and the meringue is 140–155°F.
4. Remove the bowl from heat and use a hand-held electric blender to beat the meringue until it has cooled.
5. Carefully blend the cocoa powder and slivered almonds into the mixture.
6. Cut out a circle of parchment paper about 10 in across and put it on a baking sheet. Spoon the meringue onto the paper, using a palette knife to spread it evenly.
7. Bake in the center of the oven for about 55 minutes. The meringue should be slightly chewy in the center.
8. Make the topping. Beat together the cream, yogurt, and confectioner's sugar. Spread on top of the meringue.
9. Sprinkle fresh berries on top and serve immediately.

# three wonderful almond cakes

This moist almond cake is really quick and simple to make. It tastes heavenly and luxurious, just like in a patisserie. It's a perfect birthday cake!

MAKES 1 CAKE/SERVES 12

BASIC RECIPE

1 cup plus 2 tablespoons unsalted butter, softened

1 ¼ lb homemade almond paste, see recipe page 208

5 organic eggs

½ cup all-purpose flour

butter and slivered almonds for the pan

1. Preheat the oven to 350°F.
2. Beat together the butter and grated almond paste until creamy.
3. Add the eggs, one at a time, beating the mixture after each addition.
4. Carefully fold the flour into the mixture.
5. Butter a 9 in springform cake pan and coat with crushed slivered almonds. Pour in the mixture.
6. Bake in the center of the oven for about 30 minutes. Finish the cake with a topping of your choice (see variations below).

## almond cake with crème patisserie & strawberries

MAKES 1 CAKE/SERVES 12

1 almond cake, see basic recipe above

½ batch of crème patisserie, see recipe page 209

¾ cup plus 2 tablespoons heavy whipping cream

2 ¼ cups fresh strawberries

1. Prepare the almond cake and crème patisserie according to the recipes. Leave both to cool.
2. Whip the cream until it is firm and fluffy and blend it into the crème patisserie.
3. Hull and chop or slice the strawberries. Spread the crème patisserie over the cake and decorate with the strawberries.

## almond cake with elderflower & fresh berries

MAKES 1 CAKE/SERVES 12

1 almond cake, see basic recipe above

1 batch of elderflower custard, see recipe page 210

¾ cup plus 2 tablespoons heavy whipping cream

2 ¼ cups fresh berries

1. Prepare the almond cake and the elderflower custard according to the recipes. Leave both to cool.
2. Whip the cream until it is softly peaking and blend in the elderflower custard.
3. Spread the custard over the cake and decorate with the berries.

## almond tosca cake

MAKES 1 CAKE/SERVES 12

1 almond cake, see basic recipe above

¼ cup plus 2 tablespoons heavy whipping cream

¼ cup plus 2 tablespoons sugar

¼ cup plus 2 tablespoons unsalted butter

1 cup slivered almonds

1. Prepare the almond cake according to the recipe.
2. Preheat the oven to 400°F.
3. Put the cream, sugar, honey, and butter in a saucepan. Bring to the boil, stirring continuously, until the mixture starts to come away from the sides of the saucepan.
4. Stir in the slivered almonds and pour the mixture on top of the almond cake.
5. Bake for 7–10 minutes or until golden. Leave to cool in the pan.

# berry juice & buns

My friend Stephen has a lovely expression for happiness. When I call him up and ask him how he's doing, he replies, "Berry juice and buns," meaning everything's just fine. Juice made from hand-picked berries together with freshly baked buns sum up the Swedish dream of simple, honest, wholesome goodness. I've baked buns since I was knee high, and I reckon there aren't many things that can beat a warm and moist cinnamon bun. Try some of these recipes and you'll get a taste of the Swedish ideal: berry juice and buns!

# classic buns

My friend makes the best buns in town, really moist and simply irresistible. When I asked her what her secret was, she answered butter. She uses a lot of butter in the dough. I followed her advice and, yes, an instant success! The butter should be at room temperature if you are using a food processor because it will be distributed differently, which makes the dough more elastic and the finished buns wonderfully moist. It's easier to use melted butter if you're mixing the dough by hand, but try using softened butter cut into small pieces for wonderful results.

MAKES 18–24 BUNS/2 CROWNS
BASIC RECIPE

1 tablespoon cardamom pods
1 cup milk
4 tablespoons fresh yeast
1/4 cup plus 2 tablespoons sugar
1/2 teaspoon salt
1/2 cup plus 2 tablespoons unsalted butter, softened
1 organic egg
6 1/2 – 7 1/4 cups bread flour

1. Crush the cardamom pods finely in a mortar. Pour the milk into a saucepan, add the cardamon, and heat until tepid, 100°F.
2. Sprinkle the yeast into a bowl and dissolve it in the milk, sugar, salt, butter and egg,
3. Add some flour, a little at a time, and mix to a silky and elastic dough.
4. Cover with a tea towel and leave to rise for 45–60 minutes or until doubled in size.
5. Preheat the oven to 400°F.
6. Turn the dough out on to a clean, lightly floured surface and make the buns of your choice (see variations).

## blueberry buns

MAKES 24 BUNS

1 batch of classic bun dough, see basic recipe above
egg for brushing
1 handful of slivered almonds

FILLING

3/4 cup plus 2 tablespoons unsalted butter, softened
1/2 cup demerara sugar
1 tablespoon ground cinnamon
1 cup fresh or frozen blueberries
3 tablespoons confectioner's sugar
3 tablespoons cornstarch

1. Prepare the dough according to the basic recipe.
2. Mix together the butter, demerara sugar, and cinnamon until creamy.
3. Divide the dough in half. Roll out one portion on a lightly floured surface to about a half-inch thick. Spread half the flavored butter over the dough.
4. Mix the berries with the confectioner's sugar and cornstarch in a bowl. Sprinkle half of the berries over the dough.
5. Roll up the dough as you would a Swiss roll and cut it into pieces about 2 in thick. Repeat with the remaining dough and berries.
6. Place in paper liners in a muffin tin or on a baking sheet.
7. Preheat the oven to 400°F.
8. Leave the buns to rise uncovered for 45–60 minutes or until they have doubled in size.
9. Brush with beaten egg and sprinkle slivered almonds on top. Bake in the lower part of the oven for 10 minutes or until golden brown.

## apple & almond crown

MAKES 2 CROWNS

1 batch of classic bun dough, see basic
    recipe page 132

egg for brushing

1 of handful slivered almonds

FILLING

³/₄ cup plus 2 tablespoons unsalted
    butter, softened

¹/₂ cup demerara sugar

1 tablespoon ground cinnamon

7 oz homemade almond paste, see
    recipe page 208

2 ripe apples

1. Prepare the dough according to the basic recipe.
2. Mix together the butter, demerara sugar, cinnamon, and almond paste until creamy.
3. Divide in half. Roll out one portion on a lightly floured surface to a rectangle about 8 x 12 in and one-half in thick.
4. Spread half of the filling over the dough and sprinkle one grated apple on top. Roll up the dough as you would a Swiss roll and form it into a ring.
5. Butter two 9 in springform cake tins or line two baking sheets with parchment paper. Put the dough in a cake tin or on a baking sheet.
6. Cut through the dough, almost to the bottom, at intervals of about one-half in and fold the pieces alternately in and out. Repeat with the remaining ingredients.
7. Preheat the oven to 350°F.
8. Leave the rolls to rise under a tea towel for about 1 hour.
9. Brush with beaten egg and sprinkle slivered almonds on top. Bake for about 20 minutes.

## american sticky buns

MAKES 20 BUNS

1 batch of classic bun dough, see basic
    recipe page 132

butter for the tin

egg for brushing

pecan nuts

demerara sugar

FILLING

¹/₂ cup pecan nuts

¹/₂ cup walnuts

1 cup plus 2 tablespoons unsalted
    butter, softened

¹/₂ cup brown sugar

1 tablespoon ground cinnamon

³/₄ cup raisins

CREAM CHEESE GLAZE

³/₄ cup plus 2 tablespoons cream
    cheese

3 tablespoons golden syrup or light corn
    syrup

³/₄ cup confectioner's sugar

zest of 2 limes

juice of 1 lime

1. Prepare the dough according to the basic recipe.
2. Crush the nuts coarsely in a pestle and water and mix with the butter, brown sugar, cinnamon, and raisins to a smooth paste.
3. Roll out the dough on a lightly floured surface to a large rectangle. Spread the filling over the dough. Roll up the dough tightly as you would a Swiss roll and cut it into slices about three-fourths in thick.
4. Place the buns, seam side down, on a buttered baking sheet. Use your thumb to press down in the center of the buns.
5. Preheat the oven to 400°F.
6. Leave the buns to rise under a tea towel for 45–60 minutes or until they have doubled in size.
7. Brush the buns with beaten egg and sprinkle pecan nuts and demerara sugar on top.
8. Bake in the center of the oven for about 10 minutes.
9. Mix together the cream cheese, syrup, and confectioner's sugar and add the lime zest and juice.
10. Beat the mixture with a hand-held beater until fluffy.
11. Drizzle the glaze over the buns when they have cooled a little.
12. Leave to cool completely and then pull the buns apart.

## cardamom buns

These buns will turn out moister if you make a filling by mixing together butter, sugar and cinnamon instead of simply sprinkling the spices and sugar directly onto the dough because they will absorb the butter. If you brush your buns with diluted syrup after baking they will look extra shiny and tempting.

MAKES 18 BUNS

1 batch of classic bun dough, see basic
    recipe page 132
egg for brushing
golden syrup and water for brushing
1/2 tablespoon cardamom pods
3 1/2 tablspoons sugar

FILLING

3/4 cup plus 2 tablespoons unsalted
    butter, softened
1/4 cup plus 3 tablespoons sugar
1 tablespoon ground cinnamon

1. Prepare the dough according to the basic recipe.
2. Mix together the butter, sugar, and cinnamon to make a smooth paste.
3. Divide the dough in half and roll out one portion to a rectangle about one-half in thick.
4. Spread half the filling over the dough and fold the dough in half, long edges together.
5. Cut the sheet into strips about 1 1/2 in wide and cut almost all the way along the strips (they should look like a pair of pants).
6. Twist the "pant legs" in different directions and tie them in a knot. Make sure the ends are underneath the knot. Place the buns on a baking sheet lined with parchment paper.
7. Preheat the oven to 400°F.
8. Leave the buns to rise under a tea towel for about 40 minutes until doubled in size. Brush with beaten egg and bake in the center of the oven for about 10 minutes or until golden.
9. Brush the still-warm buns with syrup mixed with water and sprinkle with ground cardamom mixed with sugar.

## vanilla buns

You can also make these plain, without any filling, or fill them with apple sauce, cloudberry, or blueberry jam.

MAKES 18 BUNS

1 batch of classic bun dough, see basic
    recipe page 132
1 batch of crème patisserie, see recipe
    page 209
butter for brushing
caster sugar

1. Prepare the dough and crème patisserie according to the basic recipes.
2. Divide the dough into 18 pieces and roll each into a ball. Put the balls on a baking sheet lined with parchment paper.
3. Flatten them a bit and leave to rise under a tea towel for about 45–60 minutes until doubled in size.
4. Preheat the oven to 400°F.
5. Put the crème patisserie in a piping bag with a round nozzle, and pipe some into each bun.
6. Bake in the center of the oven for about 7–8 minutes or until golden. Leave to cool a little.
7. Brush the buns with melted butter and roll them in sugar.

# swedish semlor

### MAKES 18 BUNS
1 batch of classic bun dough, see basic
   recipe page 132
egg for brushing
confectioner's sugar

### FILLING
14 oz homemade almond paste, see
   recipe page 208
milk
3 cups heavy whipping cream

1. Prepare the dough according to the basic recipe.
2. Divide the dough into 18 pieces and roll each into a ball.
3. Put the balls on a baking sheet lined with parchment paper.
4. Preheat the oven to 400°F.
5. Leave the buns to rise under a tea towel for about 45–60 minutes.
6. Brush the buns with beaten egg and bake in the center of the oven for about 6–7 minutes. Leave to cool.
7. Cut the tops off the buns and scoop out the insides.
8. Grate the almond paste and mix with the dough from inside the buns and sufficient milk to make a creamy paste.
9. Stuff the pastries with the filling, pipe whipped cream on top, and put the tops back on. Dust the pastries with confectioner's sugar.

# bun crackers

Dry buns can be used for two things. Either butter them and throw them on the grill like bruschetta, or make really tasty Bun Crackers. These crackers are delicious crumbled on top of vanilla ice cream or dunked in coffee.

MAKES ABOUT 30 CRACKERS
1 batch of dry cinnamon buns,
   or one crown
butter or margarine for brushing

1. Preheat the oven to 300°F.
2. Cut each bun into slices about one-half in thick.
3. Brush the slices with melted butter or margarine.
4. Place the slices on baking sheets lined with parchment paper and cook in the center of the oven for about 25 minutes until crisp.

# brioche pizza with berries

French brioche might not be the healthiest bread you can eat, but it is a real treat and makes wonderful sweet pizzas!

**MAKES 16 PIZZAS**

1 batch of brioche dough,
   see recipe page 172
1 batch of crème patisserie,
   see recipe page 209
4 ripe nectarines
2 cups fresh blackberries or raspberries
egg for brushing
demerara sugar

1. Prepare the brioche dough and crème patisserie according to the recipes.
2. Put the dough on a lightly floured surface and roll out gently to a large square. Cut the dough into 16 pieces.
3. Roll each piece into a thin circle and transfer to baking sheets lined with parchment paper.
4. Leave the pizzas to rise for 1 hour or until doubled in size.
5. Preheat the oven to 400°F.
6. Pipe a spiral of crème patisserie in the center of each pizza and top with sliced nectarines and blackberries.
7. Brush the edges with beaten egg and sprinkle some demerara sugar on top. Bake in the center of the oven for about 8–10 minutes or until golden. Leave to cool on a wire rack.

# traditional blackcurrant juice

This is a wonderful and simple juice to make if you have a lot of berries in the garden. The hardest work is probably picking the fruit.

**MAKES 7 CUPS**

4 1/2 cups fresh blackcurrants
5 cups water
1 cup plus 3 tablespoons sugar
1 teaspoon citric acid

1. Rinse the currants thoroughly.
2. Put the fruit in a large stainless steel saucepan and crush them lightly with a potato masher. Add 5 cups water and boil, uncovered, for 10 minutes. Skim off any scum.
3. Strain the juice and add the sugar and citric acid. Return to the saucepan.
4. Stir in the remaining water and slowly bring to a boil again. Skim if necessary.
5. Fill two sterilized bottles to the very top and seal.
6. Store the bottles in a cool place and mix with water to the strength you like, something around one part juice to four parts water.

# lovely lemon lemonade

This lemonade is reminiscent of the 1950s and American housewives. It's a deliciously refreshing drink and takes only a couple of minutes to whip up.

SERVES 4

juice of 8 lemons

juice of 4 limes

3/4 cups sugar

2 cups plus 2 tablespoons ice cold water
   or table water

ice cubes and slices of lemon for serving

1. Mix the lemon and lime juices with the sugar in a large jug. Stir to dissolve the sugar.
2. Add the cold water, ice cubes, and thinly sliced lemon.

# blueberry juice

This recipe is for the enthusiastic berry pickers. Nothing can compare with homemade blueberry juice. It's so simple to make, it almost takes care of itself.

MAKES 7 CUPS

4 cups fresh or frozen blueberries

5 cups water

2 3/4 cups sugar

3 teaspoons citric acid

1. Remove any stalks and rinse the blueberries carefully. Thaw the berries if you are using frozen.
2. Mash the berries with a potato masher in a bowl or mix them lightly in a blender.
3. Put the berriers in a non-metallic bowl. Add 5 cups water, stir, and cover with plastic wrap. Leave in a cool place and stir from time to time.
4. Transfer to a large saucepan, add the remaining water, and bring to a boil, stirring occasionally. Skim if necessary.
5. Strain the juice and add sugar and citric acid.
6. Pour the juice into sterilized bottles up to the very top and seal carefully.
7. Store the bottles in a cool place and mix with water to the strength you like, but around one part juice to four parts water.

# elderberry juice

Many people don't realize what a treasure elderberries can be if you use them to make this fantastic juice. Be careful not to mix up common elder with the poisonous red-berried elder or dwarf elder. Common elderberries are black and the trees bloom in early summer while the red-berried elder flowers bloom in late spring.

MAKES 7 CUPS

5 cups ripe elderberries
3 teaspoons citric acid
5 cups water
1/2 cup sugar

1. Rinse the berries and put them in a non-metallic bowl. Mash them with a potato masher.
2. Stir in the citric acid and 3 cups water.
3. Cover the bowl with a plate and leave in a cool place for about 24 hours.
4. Transfer the berries to a saucepan, add the remaining water, and bring to a boil, skimming if necessary.
5. Strain the juice and add the sugar. Bring the juice to a boil again, stir, and skim if necessary.
6. Pour the juice into sterilized bottles up to the very top and seal carefully.
7. Store the bottles in a cool place and mix with water to the strength you like, but around one part juice to four parts water.

# elderflower juice

Citric acid exists in a variety of fruits and is extracted from green lemons. In juice, jam, and preserves citric acid is used as a preservative and to control the acidity. The citric acid and the sugar together help the pectin in the fruit to set, which is why it is added to jams and pieserves.

MAKES 7 CUPS

45 clusters fresh elderflowers
zest and juice of 3 lemons
5 cups water
3/4 cup sugar
4 teaspoons citric acid

1. Place the elderflowers in a bowl and add lemon zest and juice.
2. Bring the water to a boil and stir in sugar and citric acid. Pour the liquid over the flowers.
3. Cover the bowl with a plate and leave in a cool place for three days. Stir a few times a day.
4. Boil and strain the juice.
5. Pour the juice into sterilized bottles up to the very top and seal carefully.
6. Store the bottles in a cool place and mix with water to the strength you like, but around one part juice to four parts water.

At the end of the summer, Swedish people pick up their wicker baskets and head for the forests to harvest blueberries, lingonberries, and other local specialities. Try my blueberry buns for a taste of Sweden. We should all make the most of what nature has to offer and use what's at hand in our gardens. Pick blackberries and mix them with a little melted sugar to keep in the freezer—they make a wonderful jam completely free of additives. Perfect on your morning toast or cereal!

# strawberry juice

Serve this strawberry juice chilled with ice cubes and decorated with fresh strawberries and slices of lime. It's the best party juice in the world.

MAKES 7 CUPS
4 1/2 cups strawberries
zest and juice of 2 lemons
1 vanilla pod
2 cups plus 2 tablespoons water
1 3/4 cups sugar
2 teaspoons citric acid

1. Hull and rinse the strawberries. Wash the lemons and peel them with a potato peeler.
2. Halve the vanilla pod lengthways and scrape out the seeds. Chop the strawberries and put them in a stainless steal saucepan with the vanilla seeds and lemon zest and juice.
3. Cover and boil for about 10 minutes. Mash the strawberries against the side of the saucepan and strain the juice through a fine sieve.
4. Return to the saucepan and bring to a boil. Add the sugar and citric acid and stir until the sugar has melted.
5. Pour the juice into sterilized bottles up to the very top and seal carefully.
6. Store the bottles in a cool place and mix with water to the strength you like, but around one part juice to four parts water.

# rhubarb juice

If you have a lot of rhubarb growing in your garden, this is an excellent way to use it up. The juice is really simple to make and has a wonderful summery taste.

MAKES 7 CUPS
6 cups rhubarb sticks
5 cups water
2 cups sugar
2 teaspoons citric acid
juice of 2 lemons

1. Rinse and cut the rhubarbs into small pieces. Put the rhubarb in a saucepan, add the water, and boil for about 15 minutes. Don't stir or the juice will be cloudy.
2. Strain the juice and throw away the rhubarb.
3. Return the juice to the saucepan, bring back to a boil, and add the sugar, citric acid, and lemon juice. Leave to cool.
4. Pour the juice into sterilized bottles up to the very top and seal carefully.
5. Store the bottles in a cool place and mix with water to the strength you like, but around one part juice to four parts water.

# savory bread

For those who are lovers of life there are many ways to indulge your passion. How about a luxurious breakfast in bed? Or why not while away a rainy afternoon with scrumptious teacakes and cheese? Perhaps you'd fancy a picnic in the countryside, lazing under a tree in the sun? And remember, with just one bite, you could be whisked off to Italy or Risence! None of this is hard to do: All these bread recipes are simple, and part of the fun is trying out the endless variations.

# carrot bread with walnuts

This lovely pull-apart bread is a perfect picnic treat. The spices and the carrots, added for extra moisture, make the bread extra tasty. The salt in the bread has an important function. It strengthens the gluten threads from the flour that keeps the dough together and makes it elastic while it rises. It also gives the bread a crust with a slightly darker color and a better flavor. Use sea salt if you can; it has a fuller taste.

MAKES 1 LARGE LOAF

1 cup milk

1 cup freshly squeezed carrot juice

1 1/2 teaspoons dry yeast

1/4 cup golden syrup or light corn syrup

1/4 cup plus 2 tablespoons unsalted butter, softened

1 tablespoon salt or sea salt

2 teaspoons ground cloves

2 teaspoons ground ginger

3 1/4 cups carrots

1 cup walnuts

about 7 1/2 cups bread flour

poppy seeds, pumpkin seeds, and flaked salt

1. Warm the milk and juice until they are tepid (100°F).
2. Add the liquid, syrup, butter, salt, and spices.
3. Peel and grate the carrots finely. Chop the walnuts coarsely and blend them into the mixture.
4. Add 4 cups of the flour and the yeast and then add the remainder a little at a time. Knead to make a smooth, elastic dough.
5. Cover the bowl with a tea towel and leave the dough to rise for about 45 minutes or until doubled in size.
6. Turn the dough out on to a floured surface and divide it into three equal portions.
7. Shape one piece into a round loaf and put in the center of a baking sheet lined with greaseproof paper.
8. Divide all the remaining dough into 14 pieces and shape each piece into a round ball.
9. Place the balls in a circle around the large loaf, positioning them about one-half in apart.
10. Preheat the oven to 400°F.
11. Leave the bread to rise under a tea towel for 30–40 minutes.
12. Brush the bread with water and sprinkle seeds and salt on top.
13. Bake in the bottom of the oven for about 30 minutes or until dark golden. Leave to cool on a wire rack.

# tortano

Tortano is a fabulous Italian bread filled with goodies such as prosciutto, olives, and mozzarella cheese. It's very filling and perfect for a picnic or as a meal on its own.

**MAKES 1 LOAF**

½ teaspoon dry yeast
1 cup tepid water
3 tablespoons olive oil
1 tablespoon honey
1 tablespoon flaked salt
1 cup durum wheat flour
2 ¾ cups bread flour

**FILLING**

7 oz mozzarella cheese
7 oz prosciutto
1 handful of pitted olives
1 bunch of fresh basil

1. Mix together the water, olive oil, honey, and salt.
2. Mix in the two flours and yeast a little at a time until the ingredients bind together and turn into a smooth elastic dough.
3. Cover the bowl with a tea towel and leave the dough to rise for about 30 minutes.
4. Press the dough into a rectangle about one-half in thick. Don't roll it as then the air trapped in the dough will be squeezed out.
5. Slice the mozzarella cheese and put in layers with the prosciutto, olives, and basil on top of the dough.
6. Brush the edges with water and roll up the dough as you would a Swiss roll. Shape it into a circle.
7. Preheat the oven to 500°F.
8. Put the loaf onto a baking sheet lined with greaseproof paper, dust it with flour, and leave to rise under a tea towel for about 30 minutes.
9. Put the bread in the oven, then reduce the temperature to 400°F and bake for 20–25 minutes or until golden brown.

# ciabatta classico

**MAKES 6 CIABATTAS**

1 teaspoon dry yeast
1 cup tepid water
3 tablespoons olive oil
2 teaspoons salt
¾ cup durum wheat flour
2 ¾ cups strong bread flour
olive oil for the baking sheet

1. Preheat the oven to 500°F.
2. Mix together the water and olive oil.
3. Add the salt, yeast, durum wheat flour, and the bread flour a little at a time until the ingredients bind together and turn into a smooth, elastic dough. Work the dough for 10–15 minutes with the dough hooks on your mixer.
4. Grease a baking sheet with olive oil. Shape the dough into a rectangle about three-fourths in thick. Dust the dough with flour, put it on the baking sheet, and leave it to rise under a tea towel for 30–40 minutes.
5. Divide the bread into 6 rectangles or squares and separate them a little.
6. Put the baking tin in the center of the oven. Spray some water inside the oven and bake for about 10 minutes.

# flour power

Flour is made by grinding grain. There are many different kinds, and they taste and act differently depending on exactly which type of grain you are using and how it has been ground. If it says whole wheat on the packet, the whole grain has been ground, which keeps more of the healthy nutrients in the flour.

**All-purpose** flour is made from wheat and is the most common type of flour. It is suitable for most baking and cooking.

**Bread** flour, or strong flour, is higher in protein and therefore also gluten than all-purpose flour. It can be worked more vigorously into a dough, which makes it ideal for baking bread or preparing pasta. It is not really suitable sponges or biscuits.

**Wheatgerm** flour is made from the inner part of the grain's kernel. It can be used for bread and cookies and in sauces.

**Durum wheat** flour is made from a durum wheat that has a harder protein than common wheat, making it suitable for pasta and some types of breads. Durum flour gives a full flavor and good consistency. The inner part of the durum wheat kernel is amber, which makes the flour yellowish. Bread made from durum flour has a distinctive flavor and rusks are crisper, but mix it with all-purpose flour if you are making a cake or your cake may turn out too dense.

**Buckwheat** flour is not made from a grain but from the seeds of a cereal plant. It is completely free of gluten and is therefore often used as the main ingredient in gluten-free flour.

**Graham** flour is a whole wheat flour made by grinding the kernel and its contents separately. It is often mixed with all-purpose flour to help the bread to rise. Graham flour is used to make bread and scones.

**Spelt** flour is rich in magnesium, vitamin B, and iron and can be used in cakes, but it should be combined with bread flour if being used in a dough that should rise. The gluten in spelt is more easily digested and so is easier on the stomach. Whole wheat spelt is also available.

**Cornflour** is made from ripe maize that is ground into flour. It is used to thicken sauces, pancakes, pies, and bread.

**Rye** flour is a whole grain flour where nothing is removed, which makes it into wholesome and nutritious flour, high in fibre. It is used to make dark breads with a strong rye flavor. If you want your rye bread to rise, you should add some bread flour, which will help this process.

# focaccia in seven different ways

I love this Italian bread. It's quick and simple to make and tastes lovely. There are dozens of variations, and it's the perfect bread for the party.

MAKES 2 LOAVES

BASIC RECIPE

1 ½ teaspoons dry yeast

1 cup tepid water

¼ cup olive oil

2 tablespoons honey

1 tablespoon flaked salt

4 ¼ –4 ¾ cups strong bread flour

olive oil and flaked salt for the tray and
    for the baking

1. Mix together the water, olive oil, honey, and flaked salt.
2. Mix the flour and yeast and a little at a time, working it into a dough and kneading for about 5 minutes.
3. Cover the bowl with a tea towel and leave the dough to rise for about 45 minutes or until it has doubled in size.
4. Preheat the oven to 425°F.
5. Turn out the dough onto a floured surface and divide it in two. Knead and shape each piece into a ball, then flatten to about one-half in thick.
6. Grease a baking sheet with olive oil and sprinkle with flaked salt. Put the focaccias on the baking sheet and cover with a tea towel. Leave to rise for about 30 minutes or until doubled in size.
7. Push your fingers into the dough to make holes. Drizzle generously with olive oil and sprinkle with flaked salt. Add any other flavor that you like (see variations below).
8. Bake in the center of the oven for about 10 minutes or until golden brown.

## onion focaccia

MAKES 2 LOAVES

1 batch of focaccia dough, see basic
    recipe above

3 red onions

olive oil and flaked salt for the tray
    and for the baking

1. Prepare the dough and leave it to rise on a baking sheet according to the basic recipe.
2. Peel and slice the onions thinly and arrange the onion rings on top of the dough.
3. Push your fingers into the dough to make holes. Drizzle generously with olive oil and sprinkle over flaked salt. Cook as above.

## olive & fennel focaccia

MAKES 2 LOAVES

1 batch of focaccia dough, see basic
    recipe above

7 oz pitted black olives

3 tablespoons fennel seed

olive oil and flaked salt for the tray
    and for the baking

1. Prepare the dough and leave it to rise on a baking sheet according to the basic recipe.
2. Chop the olives finely and crush the fennel seed in a mortar. Sprinkle olives and crushed fennel seed on top of the dough.
3. Push your fingers into the dough to make holes. Drizzle generously with olive oil and sprinkle over flaked salt. Cook as above.

## rosemary focaccia

MAKES 2 LOAVES

1 batch of focaccia dough, see basic
    recipe page 161
5 sprigs of rosemary
olive oil and flaked salt for the baking
    sheet and for the baking

1. Prepare the dough and leave it to rise on a baking sheet
    according to the basic recipe.
2. Crush the rosemary sprigs in a mortar. Pour some olive oil
    into the mortar and grind together with the rosemary.
3. Push your fingers into the dough to make holes. Sprinkle
    rosemary over the dough.
4. Drizzle generously with olive oil and sprinkle with flaked salt.
    Cook as above.

## potato & goat cheese focaccia

MAKES 2 LOAVES

1 batch of focaccia dough, see basic
    recipe page 161
2 large new potatoes
1 garlic clove
2 sprigs of rosemary
7 oz goat cheese, crumbled
olive oil and flaked salt for the baking
    sheet and for the baking

1. Prepare the dough and leave it to rise on a baking sheet
    according to the basic recipe.
2. Wash the potatoes and slice potatoes and garlic paper-thin.
3. Spread potatoes, garlic, some flaked salt, chopped rosemary,
    and crumbled goat cheese on top of the dough.
4. Push your fingers into the dough to make holes in the focaccia
    and make the potatoes, cheese, and garlic penetrate. Drizzle
    generously with olive oil and sprinkle with flaked salt. Cook as
    above.

## parmesan focaccia

MAKES 2 LOAVES

1 batch of focaccia dough, see basic
    recipe page 161
5 oz Parmesan cheese
olive oil and flaked salt for the baking
    sheet and for the baking

1. Prepare the dough and leave it to rise on a baking sheet
    according to the basic recipe.
2. Grate the Parmesan cheese coarsely and spread it on top of
    the dough.
3. Push your fingers into the dough to make holes. Drizzle
    generously with olive oil and sprinkle with flaked salt. Cook as
    above.

## focaccia with cherry tomatoes & basil

MAKES 2 LOAVES

1 batch of focaccia dough, see basic
    recipe page 161
1 handful cherry tomatoes, sliced
1 bunch of fresh basil
olive oil and flaked salt for the baking
    sheet and for the baking

1. Prepare the dough and leave it to rise on a baking sheet
    according to the basic recipe.
2. Push your fingers into the dough to make holes.
3. Press tomatoes and basil into the dough. Drizzle generously
    with olive oil and sprinkle with flaked salt. Cook as above.

savory bread

Is there anything better than waking up to the smell of freshly baked bread and a breakfast in bed? I love traveling and staying at a cozy hotel or bed and breakfast. A really good hotel breakfast is high on my list of priorities so I choose my destinations and hotels carefully. Sometimes such treasures are closer to home than you may think. The morning hour yields golden flour.

# baguettes

We associate the baguette with France, but actually the French didn't start to bake it until the 1920s. That was when Austrian journeymen brought a Polish method using sourdough to France and started to use this for baking baguettes. The approach gives the baguette its typical light structure containing large air bubbles.

MAKES 4 LOAVES
1 teaspoon dry yeast
1 cup cold water
3 cups bread flour
vegetable oil for the baking sheets
flaked salt, sesame seeds, sunflower
    seeds, pumpkin seeds, or
    poppy seeds

DOUGH 2
¼ teaspoon dry yeast
1 ¼ cups cold water
1 batch of dough 1 (see above)
1 tablespoon salt
1 tablespoon sugar
4 ¼ –4 ¾ cups bread flour

1. Mix together the yeast and flour.
2. Add the water and mix to make a smooth, soft dough.
3. Cover the bowl with plastic wrap and leave the dough to rise for at least 4 hours at room temperature, or overnight in the refrigerator.
4. Preheat the oven to 475°F.
5. Turn out the dough onto a floured surface and divide it into four. Gently press each portion into a rectangle.
6. Tuck in one of the long sides and roll up the dough. Shape the ends into points.
7. Twist the baguettes slightly and put them in a greased baguette tin or an ordinary baking sheet.
8. Leave the baguettes to rise under a tea towel for about 1 hour.
9. Brush the baguettes with water and sprinkle flaked salt and the seeds of your choice on top. Use a knife to make diagonal cuts in the surface of each loaf and immediately put the baking sheet in the center of the oven.
10. Reduce the heat when the baguettes start to color.
11. Bake for about 30 minutes. Leave to cool uncovered on a wire rack.

1. To make dough 2, crumble the yeast into a bowl and dissolve it in the water.
2. Add dough 1, the salt, sugar, and flour and mix until the ingredients bind together. Knead the dough by hand or at a low speed in a mixer for about 15 minutes.
3. Cover the bowl with a tea towel and leave to rise for about 1 ½ hours. Proceed as above.

savory bread

166

# white toast bread

This is my favorite recipe for toast bread. It is easy to make and works perfectly for canapés as well as for toasting.

MAKES 2 LOAVES

1 ½ teaspoons dry yeast

2 cups plus 2 tablespoons tepid water

2 teaspoons honey

2 teaspoons golden syrup

¼ cup plus 3 tablespoons olive oil

2 tablespoons salt

¾ cup durum wheat flour

6–6 ½ cups bread flour

butter and sesame seeds or poppy
   seeds for the bread tins

flaked salt

1. Mix together the water, honey, syrup, olive oil, and flaked salt.
2. Add the flour and yeast and mix until the ingredients bind together and make a soft, elastic dough.
3. Cover the bowl with a tea towel and leave the dough to rise for about 40 minutes or until it has doubled in size.
4. Butter and coat two bread tins with sesame seeds or poppy seeds.
5. Divide the dough in half, knead, and roll out into two loafs. Put the loaves in the bread tins.
6. Preheat the oven to 400°F.
7. Cover the tins with a tea towel and leave the loaves to rise for about 30 minutes or until they have doubled in size.
8. Brush the loaves with water, sprinkle flaked salt on top, and use a knife to score a lengthways depression down the center of each loaf.
9. Bake immediately in the center of the oven for 25–30 minutes and leave the loaves to cool on a wire rack.

# fougasse from risence

Fougasse is a large, leaf-shaped, pull-apart bread from France. It can be flavored with nuts, olives, and fresh herbs. It tastes great and is perfect to eat just as it is.

**MAKES 2 LOAVES**

1 teaspoon fresh yeast

1 cup tepid water

¼ cup plus 3 tablespoons olive oil

5 sprigs of fresh rosemary

5 sprigs of fresh thyme

1 tablespoon flaked salt

¼ cup durum wheat flour

5 cups bread flour

¾ cup pitted black olives

olive oil for brushing

flaked salt and fresh thyme

1. Mix together the water and the olive oil.
2. Chop the herbs finely and mix them with the liquid.
3. Add the flaked salt, yeast, and the two flours and mix to form a soft, elastic dough. Work the dough in a mixer for about 15 minutes.
4. Cover the bowl with a tea towel and leave the dough to rise for about 1 hour or until it has doubled in size.
5. Divide the dough in two and knead half the chopped olives into each portion.
6. Roll out the dough into ovals about three-fourths in thick. Put them on a baking sheet lined with greaseproof paper.
7. Cut "veins" in the dough to resemble leaves and gently pull the dough to open up the cuts.
8. Preheat the oven to 500°F.
9. Cover the bread with a tea towel and leave to rise for about 30 minutes or until it has doubled in size.
10. Brush the bread with olive oil, sprinkle flaked salt and fresh thyme on top, and bake immediately in the center of the oven for about 10 minutes or until golden. You will get a nice crust if you spray some water in the oven when you put in the bread.

# homemade rosemary grissini

**MAKES 30 GRISSINI**

¾ teaspoon dry yeast

½ cup tepid water

1 teaspoon salt

2 teaspoons sugar

1 organic egg white

¼ cup olive oil

2 sprigs of fresh rosemary

3 cups all-purpose flour

flaked salt and chopped rosemary

1. Stir together the water, salt, and sugar.
2. Mix the egg white, olive oil, and finely chopped rosemary into the liquid.
3. Mix together the flour and yeast. Add to wet mixture a little at a time until the dough binds together.
4. Leave the dough to rise under a tea towel for about 1 ½ hours.
5. Preheat the oven to 350°F.
6. Knead the dough on a floured surface and roll it into sticks, about the thickness of a pencil.
7. Brush the grissini with water, sprinkle with flaked salt and rosemary, and bake in the center of the oven for about 25 minutes or until they are golden brown.

savory bread

# french brioche

MAKES 20 BRIOCHES

3/4 teaspoon dry yeast

5 organic eggs

4 1/4 cups bread flour

1 teaspoon salt

1/4 cup sugar

1 1/2 cups plus 2 tablespoons
butter, softened

rape oil for the sealed plastic
container

butter for the brioche tins

egg and salt for brushing

1. Lightly beat the eggs.
2. Mix together the dry ingredients and add them to the eggs.
3. Knead with dough hooks for about 15 minutes until it is smooth and elastic.
4. Divide the butter into four and add it gradually to the dough, mixing well between each addition.
5. Lightly oil a plastic container, pour in the dough, and put on the lid. Leave the dough to rise in a warm place for about 2 hours or until it has doubled in size.
6. Knead the dough with your hands until it turns silky.
7. Return the dough to the plastic container and leave to rest in the refrigerator overnight.
8. Brush 20 small brioche tins with melted butter.
9. Roll out the dough and divide it into 20 even pieces. Put them in the tins.
10. Brush them with beaten egg mixed with salt. Be careful not to let the egg run between the dough and the tin or they will not rise.
11. Leave the dough to rise under a tea towel for about 1 hour until doubled in size.
12. Preheat the oven to 425°F.
13. Cook in the center of the oven for 8–10 minutes or until golden brown.

# pain au chocolat

MAKES 8

9 oz fresh puff pastry

1/2 cup chocolate and hazelnut
spread

1/4 cup good-quality dark chocolate
(70% cocoa solids)

3 oz homemade almond paste, see
recipe page 208

zest of 1 orange

egg for brushing

slivered almonds

icing sugar

1. Preheat the oven to 350°F.
2. Roll out the pastry on a lightly floured surface to a rectangle about one-fourth in thick. Cut it into eight rectangles.
3. Spread a dab of chocolate spread over one short side of each rectangle.
4. Chop the chocolate coarsely and grate the almond paste. Mix with the orange zest and sprinkle over the chocolate spread.
5. Roll up the pieces from the short side and put them, seam down, on a baking sheet lined with greaseproof paper.
6. Brush with whisked egg and sprinkle with slivered almonds.
7. Bake in the center of the oven for about 20 minutes or until golden.
8. Dust with icing sugar.

# my sister's teacakes

When I was a little girl, my mother and I used to drink tea and munch juicy teacakes with cheese and marmalade. You can freeze teacakes it there are any left over, but it is best to freeze them when they are freshly baked.

MAKES 10

2 cups plus 2 tablespoons milk

1 ½ cups rolled oats

½ tablespoon salt

1 tablespoon golden syrup or light corn syrup

½ cup plus 2 tablespoons unsalted butter

1 teaspoon dry yeast

4 ³⁄₄–5 ½ cups bread flour

1. Heat the milk to about 120°F and stir in the oats, salt, and syrup. Leave to swell for about 20 minutes.
2. Melt the butter and stir into mixture.
3. Gradually add the flour and yeast, mixing to make a soft dough.
4. Cover the bowl with a tea towel and leave the dough to rise for about 30 minutes or until doubled in size.
5. Preheat the oven to 425°F.
6. Knead the dough on a floured surface and form it into ten pieces, each about one-half in thick. Prick the tops with a fork and put them on a baking sheet lined with greaseproof paper. Leave to rise under a tea towel for about 30 minutes.
7. Bake in the center of the oven for about 10 minutes.

# soft flat bread

We often ate freshly-baked, soft flat breads when we were kids, and I've always had a special liking for them. Don't let them bake too long or the edges will turn hard.

MAKES 6

1 tablespoon fennel seeds

1 tablespoon aniseeds

2 teaspoons flaked salt

2 cups plus 2 tablespoons milk

3 ½ tablespoons sugar

1 ½ teaspoons dry yeast

4 ¼ cups bread flour

4 ¼ cups sifted rye flour

½ cup butter, softened

1. Crush the spices together with the salt in a mortar.
2. Heat the milk together with the spices and the sugar until tepid.
3. Crumble the yeast into a bowl and mix it with the liquid.
4. Add the flours a little at a time and work in a mixer to make a smooth, elastic dough. Add the butter and knead for about 10 minutes.
5. Cover the bowl with a tea towel and leave the dough to rise for about 1 hour or until doubled in size. Knock the dough back after about half an hour.
6. Turn the dough out on a floured surface and divide it into six. Roll each portion into a ball, then flatten them to about one-half in thick. Prick the tops with a fork and dust with flour.
7. Preheat the oven to 500°F.
8. Put the breads on a baking sheet lined with greaseproof paper and leave to rise for about 40 minutes.
9. Bake in the center of the oven for 7–8 minutes.

savory bread

# scones

This recipe is good enough for a royal tea party. You can vary the flavors endlessly. See the variations below and on the next pages.

MAKES 6
BASIC RECIPE
4 ½ cups all-purpose flour
½ teaspoon salt
1 ½ teaspoons baking powder
¼ cup demerara sugar
½ cup plus 1 tablespoon cold unsalted
    butter
1 organic egg
¾ cup plus 2 tablespoons milk
egg, slivered almonds, and demerara
    sugar for finishing

1. Preheat the oven to 450°F.
2. Mix together the flour, salt, baking powder, and sugar.
3. Dice the butter and mix it with the dry ingredients with your fingertips to make breadcrumbs.
4. Whisk the egg together with the milk.
5. Mix the liquid and dry ingredients together to make a stiff dough.
6. Turn out the dough on a lightly floured surface and roll it out to about one in thick. Use a biscuit cutter to cut out six rounds.
7. Put them on a baking sheet lined with greaseproof paper. Brush with beaten egg and sprinkle with slivered almonds and demerara sugar.
8. Bake in the center of the oven for about 10 minutes or until golden.

## blueberry & lemon scones

MAKES 6
1 batch of scone dough, see basic recipe
    above and instructions
½ cup all-purpose flour
zest of 2 lemons
⅓ cup fresh or frozen blueberries
egg and demerara sugar for finishing

1. Prepare the dough according to the basic recipe, but add additional flour and lemon zest.
2. Carefully fold the blueberries into the dough, taking care that you do not crush them.
3. Follow the instructions in the basic recipe. Brush with beaten egg and sprinkle demerara sugar on top before putting the scones in the oven.

## chocolate scones

MAKES 6
1 batch of scone dough, see basic recipe
    above and instructions
4 oz good-quality dark chocolate (70%
    cocoa solids), chopped
egg and demerara sugar for finishing

1. Prepare the dough according to the basic recipe, but add coarsely chopped chocolate.
2. Follow the instructions in the basic recipe. Brush with beaten egg and sprinkle demerara sugar on top before putting the scones in the oven.

## whole wheat scones

MAKES 6

1 batch of scone dough, see basic recipe
    page 176 and instructions

1 ¼ cups whole wheat flour (instead of
    all-purpose flour)

2 teaspoons cardamom pods

egg, poppy seeds, and demerara sugar
    for finishing

1. Prepare the dough according to the basic recipe, but use whole wheat flour instead of the all-purpose flour. Also bring the milk to the boil with the crushed cardamom pods before mixing the liquids with the dry ingredients.
2. Follow the instructions in the basic recipe. Brush with beaten egg and sprinkle poppy seeds and demerara sugar on top before putting the scones in the oven.

## strawberry scones with walnuts

MAKES 6

1 batch of scone dough, see basic recipe
    page 176 and instructions

¼ cup all-purpose flour

1 ½ cups walnuts

¾ cup fresh strawberries

egg and demerara sugar for finishing

1. Prepare the dough according to the basic recipe, but add an extra ¼ cup flour with the coarsely chopped walnuts.
2. Hull and slice the strawberries. Fold them into the dough, taking care not to crush them.
3. Follow the instructions in the basic recipe. Brush with beaten egg and sprinkle demerara sugar on top before putting the scones in the oven.

## coconut & lime scones

MAKES 6

1 batch of scone dough, see basic recipe
    page 176 and instructions

1 ⅔ cups unsweetened coconut

zest of 2 limes

egg, unsweetened coconut, and
    demerara sugar for finishing

1. Toast the coconut in a dry saucepan.
2. Prepare the dough according to the basic recipe, but add the roasted coconut and the lime zest.
3. Follow the instructions in the basic recipe. Brush with beaten egg and sprinkle unsweetened coconut and demerara sugar on top before putting the scones in the oven.

## saffron scones

MAKES 6

1 batch of scone dough, see basic recipe
    page 176 and instructions

1 pinch of saffron

egg, slivered almonds, and demerara
    sugar for finishing

1. Prepare the dough according to the basic recipe, but bring the milk to the boil together with the saffron before mixing the liquids with the dry ingredients.
2. Follow the instructions in the basic recipe. Brush with beaten egg and sprinkle slivered almonds and demerara sugar on top before putting the scones in the oven.

savory bread

## spicy raisin scones

MAKES 6

1 batch of scone dough, see basic recipe
    page 176 and instructions

1 teaspoon ground clove

2 teaspoons ground cinnamon

3/4 cup currants or raisins

egg, pumpkin seeds, and demerara
    sugar for finishing

1. Prepare the dough according to the basic recipe, but bring the milk to the boil together with the spices and the currants before mixing the liquids with the dry ingredients.
2. Follow the instructions in the basic recipe. Brush with beaten egg and sprinkle pumpkin seeds and demerara sugar on top before putting the scones in the oven.

## muesli scones with sunflower seeds

MAKES 6

1 batch of scone dough, see basic recipe
    page 176 and instructions

1/3 cup fruit muesli (instead of 1/4 cup
    all-purpose flour)

egg, sunflower seeds, and demerara
    sugar for finishing

1. Prepare the dough according to the basic recipe, but replace 1/4 cup of the flour with 1/3 cup fruit muesli.
2. Follow the instructions in the basic recipe. Brush with beaten egg and sprinkle sunflower seeds and demerara sugar on top before putting the scones in the oven.

## stilton scones with dried fruits

MAKES 6

1 batch of scone dough, see basic recipe
    page 176 and instructions

4 oz (about 1 cup crumbled) blue
    cheese, preferably Stilton

1 cup walnuts

1/2 cup dried apricots

1/2 cup dried figs

egg and demerara sugar for finishing

1. Prepare the dough according to the basic recipe, but add the crumbled blue cheese and coarsely chopped walnuts, apricots, and figs.
2. Follow the instructions in the basic recipe. Brush with beaten egg and sprinkle demerara sugar on top before putting the scones in the oven.

# hearty wholegrain & crisp bread

I love to serve a sweet, dark bread with dried fruit and nuts when I am putting together a cheese platter. The sweetness of the fruit and the saltiness of the cheese are a great combination. The quick and simple French spicy bread *pain d'épices* is my first choice as a complement to dessert cheeses, while the fruit bread, which is baked from sourdough, goes well with milder cheeses for an open sandwich. When it comes to rye breads, I have many favorites, but there are few things that beat a warm rye roll with some cheese and marmalade.

# pain d'épices

Pain d'épices is an outstanding bread for the cheese board. It is really quick and easy to make. Just mix the ingredients together and bake it.

MAKES 1 LOAF

½ cup honey
¼ cup demerara sugar
½ cup heavy whipping cream
1 teaspoon aniseeds
1 teaspoon caraway seeds
1 teaspoon coriander seeds
1 teaspoon fennel seeds
1 teaspoon ground ginger
1 teaspoon ground cinnamon
¾ cup dried apricots
⅓ cup pumpkin seeds
⅓ cup walnuts
1 ⅛ cups all-purpose flour
1 teaspoon flaked salt
2 teaspoons baking soda
butter and slivered almonds for the pan

1. Preheat the oven to 300°F.
2. Bring the honey, demerara sugar, heavy whipping cream, and the spices to the boil in a saucepan. Pour into a bowl and leave to cool.
3. Chop the apricots and mix them with the pumpkin seeds and walnuts. Add the flour, salt, and baking soda.
4. Mix the dry ingredients with the liquids.
5. Butter and coat a 9 in sponge cake pan with crushed slivered almonds. Pour the mixture into the pan. Bake in the center of the oven for 40–50 minutes or until a skewer inserted into the center comes out clean.

# classic crisp bread

My mother-in-law loves this crisp bread; it's her absolute favorite. She always selects organic products and loves wholegrain bread. This is not the coarsest kind, but it is really good and it doesn't have to rise because it uses baking soda in the dough.

MAKES 20 CRISP BREADS

2 cups plus 2 tablespoons buttermilk
½ cup golden syrup or light corn syrup
2 teaspoons fennel seeds
2 teaspoons aniseeds
About 10 cups sifted rye flour
2 teaspoons salt
2 teaspoons baking soda

1. Mix the buttermilk with the syrup.
2. Pound the fennel seeds and the aniseeds in a mortar.
3. Mix together all the dry ingredients, add the liquid, and knead into a dough.
4. Divide the dough into 20 pieces, roll them out into round cakes, and prick them with a fork.
5. Fry the cakes for about a minute on each side in a dry frying pan over a medium heat. Leave to cool on a wire rack.

Using sourdough improves the bread's texture and taste and makes it keep longer. A sourdough is made from only water and flour, and when it is left at room temperature for a while it will start producing lactic and acetic acids and a natural yeast culture. If it's looked after properly, a sourdough came become very old and I've heard of sourdoughs in Finland where they've been passed down for generations! Baking with normal yeast and sourdough at the same time is an easy and good way to start experimenting with sourdough bread at home. It might sound complicated to use sourdough but it really isn't and the result is much more satisfying than bread made with yeast alone.

# sourdough

Sometimes conventional flour is too "clean" to make a good sourdough. Organic flour isn't as refined and is better. As long as you keep the sourdough in the refrigerator it will rest. The day before you want to use it, feed it with some rye flour and water to "wake it."

MAKES 1 BATCH OF RYE
 SOURDOUGH
1 ¾ cups tepid water
3 cups organic wholegrain rye flour

MAKES 1 BATCH OF WHEAT
 SOURDOUGH
1 ¾ cups tepid water
3 cups organic wheat flour

1. Mix 1 cup water with 2 cups flour. Cover with plastic wrap and leave at room temperature for two days.
2. Add ½ cup water and ½ cup flour. Mix carefully. Cover with plastic wrap and leave at room temperature for another day.
3. Add another ¼ cup water and ½ cup flour. Mix, cover with plastic wrap, and leave at room temperature for one more day.

# fruit & hazelnut sourdough

MAKES 2 LOAVES
1 teaspoon dry yeast
¾ cup cold water
1 tablespoon molasses
2 teaspoons salt
2 teaspoons ground cinnamon
½ cup rye sourdough (optional),
 see basic recipe above
2 ½ cups wholegrain rye flour
4 ¼ cups bread flour
1 cup hazelnuts
⅔ cup raisins
1 bag of mixed dried fruits
wholegrain rye flour for baking
butter for the pans

1. Crumble the yeast in a bowl and add the water, molasses, salt, and cinnamon.
2. Add the sourdough (if using), rye flour, and some all-purpose flour a little at a time and knead slowly in a food processor until the dough is elastic.
3. Work the dough for about 5 minutes at a higher speed and add the whole hazelnuts, raisins, and coarsely chopped dried fruits.
4. Leave the dough to rise under a tea towel for about 1 hour or until doubled in size.
5. Put an empty roasting pan at the bottom of the oven and preheat the oven to 475°F.
6. Divide the dough in two. Fold the dough a couple of times and shape loaves. Roll the loaves in wholegrain rye flour and put in two buttered rectangular loaf pans. Leave to rise under a tea towel for about 1 hour.
7. Using a sharp knife, carefully score three cuts lengthways before putting the loaves in the oven. Pour ¾ coffee cup water in the hot roasting pan and close the oven door quickly. Lower the heat to 450°F and bake the bread for about 30 minutes.
8. Lift the bread out of the pans and leave to cool on a wire rack.

# danish rye bread

This bread is even better if you leave it for a day before eating it. It's very moist and lasts well: it will keep in a plastic bag for 1–2 weeks.

MAKES 3 LOAVES

STARTER

3 tablespoons fennel seeds

3 tablespoons aniseeds

3 tablespoons ground caraway seeds

3 tablespoons salt

2 cups boiling water

3 1/2 cups rye grits

5 tablespoons linseeds

DOUGH

2 teaspoons dry yeast

2 cups plus 2 tablespoons tepid water

1 cup molasses

1 cup sunflower seeds

1/3 cup pumpkin seeds

6 1/2 cups wholegrain rye flour

4 1/4 cups bread flour

1. Grind the fennel seeds and aniseeds in a mortar. Mix all the ingredients for the starter in a bowl. Cover with plastic wrap and leave at room temperature for 1–3 days.
2. Crumble the yeast into a bowl. Add the water and the molasses.
3. Stir the starter into the bowl.
4. Blend in the sunflower seeds, pumpkin seeds, and add the flour a little at a time. The dough should be very sticky.
5. Knead with dough hooks in a food processor for about 30 minutes. The dough should still be sticky.
6. Preheat the oven to 475°F.
7. Line rectangular bread pans with greaseproof paper and fill with the dough. Sprinkle some rye flour on top and leave the bread to rise for about 30 minutes.
8. Use a knife to make lengthways cuts in the top of each loaf and bake in the lower part of the oven for about 1 1/2 hours. Use a vaporiser to spray water into the oven during the baking (once or twice) to give the bread a good crust.
9. Cover the bread with foil after about 30 minutes to prevent the loaves from turning too dark.
10. Remove the bread from the pans and leave to cool on a wire rack.

# sporty brown rolls

Use a measuring cup for measuring the flour for these healthy rolls. Pour the flour into the measuring cup until you reach the required weight. If you scoop the flour from the bag with a small measuring spoon the flour might become too tightly packed and you will end up with more flour than is necessary for the dough.

MAKES 30 SMALL ROLLS
STARTER
2 cups plus 2 tablespoons boiling water
2 1/2 teaspoons aniseeds
2 1/2 teaspoons caraway seeds
2 1/2 teaspoons coriander seeds
2 1/2 teaspoons fennel seeds
3 tablespoons salt
3/4 cup rye grits
2/3 cup crushed linseeds
1 1/3 cups plus 2 tablespoons rye flour
1 3/4 cups spelt

DOUGH
2 cups plus 2 tablespoons milk
1 1/2 teaspoons dry yeast
3/4 cup molasses
1 cup hazelnuts
1 1/4 cups high-fiber rolled oats
1/2 cup raisins
1/2 cup dried apricots
1/2 cup dried figs
1 1/2 cups rye flour
1 3/4 cups spelt flour
3 1/3 cups bread flour
sunflower seeds

1. Mix all the ingredients for the starter in a bowl. Cover with plastic wrap and leave the mixture to swell at room temperature for at least 30 minutes.
2. Heat the milk to tepid, 100°F.
3. Pour the yeast into a bowl and stir in the milk.
4. Add the starter to the bowl and stir to combine.
5. Blend in the molasses, hazelnuts, rolled oats, raisins, chopped apricots, and chopped figs.
6. Add the flour a little at a time. The dough should be really sticky.
7. Drop the buns onto a baking sheet lined with greaseproof paper and sprinkle sunflower seeds and flour on top.
8. Preheat the oven to 400°F.
9. Leave the buns to rise under a tea towel for about 1 1/2 hours.
10. Bake in the center of the oven for about 20 minutes.

# morning glory rolls

These rolls are perfect at breakfast time. Eat them freshly baked with butter and Cheddar cheese.

MAKES 14 ROLLS

1 teaspoon dry yeast
1 teaspoon caraway seeds
1 teaspoon aniseeds
1/4 cup butter
3 tablespoons honey
1 cup cold water
5 tablespoons sunflower seeds
5 tablespoons pumpkin seeds
2 teaspoons salt
1/2 cup wholegrain spelt flour
1/2 cup whole wheat flour
1 cup all-purpose spelt flour
2 1/3–3 1/2 cups bread flour
egg for brushing
flaked salt, sunflower seeds, and
    pumpkin seeds

1. Put the yeast into a bowl.
2. Pound the caraway seeds and the aniseeds in a mortar.
3. Melt together the butter, spices, and honey. Remove from the heat and add the water. Pour the liquid over the yeast.
4. Toast the sunflower and pumpkin seeds with the flaked salt in a dry saucepan. Add the liquid and stir.
5. Mix in the flour a little at a time and work the dough until it starts to come away from the sides of the bowl. It should be a bit sticky.
6. Work the dough slowly in a food processor for about 20 minutes.
7. Cover with a tea towel and leave to rise for about 45 minutes or until doubled in size.
8. Preheat the oven to 400°F.
9. Turn out the dough onto a floured surface and divide it into 14 pieces. Transfer the rolls to a baking sheet lined with greaseproof paper and leave to rise for about 1 hour.
10. Brush the buns with beaten egg, sprinkle flaked salt, sunflower seeds, and pumpkin seeds on top.
11. Bake in the center of the oven for about 10 minutes.

# sweet rye & raisin rolls

If you use stone-ground flour you need to add more water than if you are using conventional flour. Organic stone-ground flour gives the buns a richer taste.

MAKES 12 ROLLS

2 1/2 tablespoons butter
1 cup milk
1/4 cup molasses
1 teaspoon salt
1 teaspoon aniseeds
1 teaspoon caraway seeds
1 teaspoon coriander seeds
1 teaspoon fennel seeds
1 1/2 teaspoons dry yeast
1/2 cup raisins
2 1/4 cups rye flour
2 3/4 cups bread flour

1. Melt the butter and add the milk, molasses, salt, and seeds.
2. Warm the liquid to tepid, 100°F.
3. Dissolve the yeast in the liquid.
4. Stir in the raisins and some of the flours a little at a time to give a smooth dough.
5. Cover the bowl with a tea towel and leave the dough to rise for about 30 minutes or until doubled in size.
6. Preheat the oven to 425°F.
7. Divide the dough into 12 pieces and dip them in sifted rye flour. Put them on a baking sheet lined with greaseproof paper and leave to rise for about 30 minutes.
8. Bake in the center of the oven for about 10 minutes.

# honey & buttermilk bread

I invented this wonderful bread one day in a summer cottage. It's definitely a family favorite.

MAKES 2 LOAVES

¼ cup butter

2 cups plus 2 tablespoons buttermilk

1 ½ teaspoons dry yeast

¾ cup plus 2 tablespoons molasses

2 teaspoons salt

5–5 ½ cups bread flour

1 ⅔ cups rye flour

1. Melt the butter and mix with the buttermilk. Warm until tepid, 100°F.
2. Pour the yeast into a bowl and add the liquid, molasses, and salt.
3. Add the bread flour and rye flour a little at a time until the dough binds together and becomes soft and elastic. Knead in the last of the flour by hand.
4. Cover the bowl with a tea towel and leave the dough to rise until doubled in size.
5. Preheat the oven to 400°F.
6. Knead and shape the dough into two loaves and put them in floured bread pans or on a baking sheet lined with greaseproof paper. Cover with a tea towel and leave to rise for about 40 minutes.
7. Bake in the center of the oven for 35–40 minutes. Cover with foil after 20 minutes to prevent the bread from over-browning.

# aunt sally's cranberry & raisin bread

When I was a child, we often baked this juicy wholegrain cranberry bread. We all loved it, and it's still one of my favorites.

MAKES 2 LOAVES

1 ¾ cups warm water

¾ cup plus 2 tablespoons cranberry jam

¼ cup plus 3 tablespoons olive oil

¼ cup golden syrup or light corn syrup

1 teaspoon vinegar

1 tablespoon salt

1 tablespoon caraway seeds

1 tablespoon fennel seeds

1 cup raisins

5 tablespoons linseeds

2 ½ teaspoons dry yeast

1 cup whole wheat flour

1 ⅓ cups rye flour

6–6 ½ cups bread flour

1. Mix the warm water, about 105°F, cranberry jam, olive oil, syrup, vinegar, and salt. Pound spices in a mortar and mix with raisins and linseeds in a bowl.
2. Mix the dry yeast with the wholegrain flour, the rye flour, and the bread flour. Stir into the liquid a little at a time until the dough binds together. It should be sticky.
3. Cover with a tea towel and leave to rise for about 1 hour or until doubled in size.
4. Knead and shape into two loaves and put them on a baking sheet lined with greaseproof paper or in greased rectangular bread pans.
5. Preheat the oven to 350°F.
6. Cover with a tea towel and leave to rise for about 1 ½ hours.
7. Bake in the center of the oven for about 40 minutes or until golden.

# delicious rye rolls

This was one of the first recipes I learned during my time in the restaurant business. It has always been one of my favorites.

MAKES 4 ROLL CAKES

1/4 cup butter
1/4 cup olive oil
1 3/4 cups milk
1/4 cup plus 3 tablespoons molasses
2 teaspoons salt
1 teaspoon aniseeds
1 teaspoon caraway seeds
1 teaspoon coriander seeds
1 teaspoon fennel seeds
2 1/2 teaspoons dry yeast
1 1/2 cups rye flour
1 teaspoon vinegar
5-5 1/2 cups bread flour

1. Melt the butter in a saucepan. Add the olive oil, milk, molasses, salt, and seeds and heat to about 115°F.
2. Mix the dry yeast and rye flour in a bowl and pour in the liquid. Add vinegar and knead.
3. Add the bread flour a little at a time and mix until the dough starts to come away from the sides of the bowl.
4. Cover with a tea towel and leave to rise for about 1 hour or until doubled in size.
5. Turn out the dough onto a floured surface. Knead and shape into four round cakes and score a cross on top of each one.
6. Put them on a baking sheet lined with greaseproof paper and prick with a fork.
7. Preheat the oven to 400°F.
8. Cover with a tea towel and rise for about 30 minutes.
9. Bake in the center of the oven for about 15 minutes.

# potato flatbread

MAKES 20 FLATBREADS

1/4 teaspoon dry yeast
1 teaspoon aniseeds
1 teaspoon fennel seeds
1 1/2 teaspoons salt
1/4 cup butter
1 cup milk
3 tablespoons golden syrup or light corn syrup
3 tablespoons sugar
3/4 cup rye flour
2 1/2 cups bread flour

FILLING

1 1/2 cups warm, freshly boiled peeled potatoes
1 cup sifted rye flour (see above)
1 cup bread flour

1. Put the yeast into a bowl.
2. Crush the seeds together with the salt in a mortar.
3. Melt the butter and heat it with the milk, syrup, sugar, and crushed seeds until tepid, 100°F.
4. Pour the liquid over the yeast and stir thoroughly.
5. Add the flour a little at a time and stir to make a sticky dough.
6. Cover with a tea towel and leave to rise for about 1 hour or until doubled in size.
7. Mash the boiled potatoes with a fork and knead them into the dough. Add the rye flour and bread flour and mix to make a smooth dough.
8. Divide into 20 pieces and roll into thin round cakes. Prick them with a fork.
9. Fry the cakes for about a minute on each side until they get a little color in a dry frying pan at medium heat. Be careful not to fry too long or the cakes will turn hard.

# traditional swedish crisp bread

I often bake these crisp breads for the cheeseboard and for midsummer parties. They should be really brittle and crisp, so roll the dough as thinly as possible.

MAKES 24 CRISP BREADS

2 cups plus 2 tablespoons milk

1/2 tablespoon honey

1/2 tablespoon golden syrup or light corn syrup

1 teaspoon salt

1 teaspoon fennel seeds

1 teaspoon caraway seeds

1/8 teaspoon dry yeast

1 cup plus 2 tablespoons all-purpose flour

2 cups rye flour

3 cups whole wheat flour

1. Heat the milk with the honey, syrup, salt, and ground seeds, until tepid, 100°F.
2. Crumble the yeast into a bowl and dissolve it in the liquid.
3. Add the flour a little at a time and work into an elastic dough.
4. Preheat the oven to 425°F.
5. Cover with a tea towel and leave to rise for about 1 hour.
6. Turn the dough out on a lightly floured surface and roll out thinly. Cut out about 24 breads and put them on baking sheets lined with greaseproof paper.
7. Bake in the center of the oven for 3–4 minutes or until the breads begin to color, turn them over, and bake for another minute.

# vanilla & poppy seed crisp bread

Brush the bread with beaten egg and sprinkle poppy seeds and black pepper on top. Sometimes I use other seeds, like pumpkin seeds or sesame seeds. It's a perfect snack to enjoy with a drink.

MAKES 30 CRISP BREADS

1 vanilla pod

1/2 cup water

1 teaspoon honey

1 teaspoon salt

1 3/4 teaspoons dry yeast

3 tablespoons poppy seeds

1 tablespoon olive oil

1 cup plus 2 tablespoons all-purpose flour

3/4 cup rye flour

1. Halve the vanilla pod lengthways and scrape out the seeds. Bring the water, vanilla seeds, honey, and salt to the boil.
2. Leave to cool until tepid, 100°F. Strain out the vanilla seeds.
3. Put the yeast in a bowl and dissolve it in the liquid.
4. Add the poppy seeds and olive oil.
5. Add the flour a little at a time and work into an elastic dough.
6. Preheat the oven to 400°F.
7. Cover with a tea towel and leave to rise for about 1 hour.
8. Turn the dough out on a lightly floured surface and roll it out thinly. Cut out about 30 breads and put them on a baking sheets lined with greaseproof paper.
9. Bake in the center of the oven for 3–4 minutes until the breads begin to color, turn them over, and bake for another minute.

# turbo fast buttermilk bread

This really quick and healthy bread is a favorite with all my friends. I vary this recipe, sometimes adding nuts, like almonds, walnuts, or pecan nuts. At other times I make it with dried fruit. You can't find an easier bread made with baking powder.

MAKES 1 LOAF

1 1/2 cups buttermilk

1/4 cup plus 3 tablespoons molasses

1/2 cup dried apricots or figs

1/3 cup hazelnuts

1/2 cup raisins

1/2 cup rye grits

2 tablespoons rolled oats

1 1/2 cups plus 3 tablespoons rye flour

1 3/4 cups all-purpose flour

5 tablespoons crushed linseeds

5 tablespoons sunflower seeds

1 1/2 teaspoons salt

1 1/2 teaspoons baking powder

1 1/2 teaspoons baking soda

1/2 teaspoon aniseeds

1/2 teaspoon caraway seeds

1/2 teaspoon coriander seeds

1/2 teaspoon fennel seeds

rolled oats

1. Preheat the oven to 400°F.
2. Mix the buttermilk and the syrup in a bowl.
3. Chop the fruit and the hazelnuts really coarsely, mix with the raisins and the dry ingredients. Stir into the buttermilk.
4. Line a loaf pan with greaseproof paper, leaving the excess paper to overlap at the ends and sides.
5. Pour the mixture into the pan, sprinkle some rolled oats on top, and bake in the center of the oven for about 45 minutes.

# baking without an oven

Sometimes I get a strong urge to bake something only to realize that I do not have an oven at hand! I may be on holiday somewhere or perhaps my own oven has finally given up the ghost. This is a great opportunity to choose one of the following recipes that rely on cold rather than heat to finish them off.

## chocolate marzipan log

This was originally a way of using up dry cakes in the baker's shop. They usually mix both sponge crumbs and cake crumbs together, and I think this is a wonderful way of using a sponge that has gone dry.

MAKES 18 SMALL LOGS

1/4 cup unsalted butter, softened
3/4 cup crumbs from cookies or graham crackers
2 teaspoons good-quality cocoa powder
arrack liquor or your favorite liquor for flavor
11 oz green marzipan and green food coloring
confectioner's sugar for rolling
4 oz good-quality dark chocolate (70% cocoa solids)

1. Mix together the butter and the crumbs until creamy and stir in cocoa powder.
2. Add the liquor of your choice.
3. Divide the dough into three pieces and roll them into long sausages. Put them in the freezer.
4. Divide the marzipan into three and shape into sausages then roll out as thinly as possible. If the marzipan becomes sticky, dust it with icing sugar.
5. Take the dough out of the freezer and roll the marzipan around them. Make sure the joins overlap and are underneath the biscuits. Put the biscuits back into the freezer.
6. Melt one-third of the chocolate in a bowl set over a pan of simmering water. Remove the bowl from the pan as soon as the chocolate has melted.
7. Chop and add the remaining chocolate. Stir until it has melted. Leave to cool.
8. Take the rolls out of the freezer and cut them into 2 in pieces. Dip the ends in the chocolate. Store the logs in the refrigerator.

## cognac bomb

MAKES 20

1/2 cup unsalted butter, softened
1/3 cup sugar
1 1/4 cups rolled oats
4 tablespoons good-quality cocoa powder
3 tablespoons cold coffee
arrack liquor or cognac
chocolate sprinkles

1. Mix together the butter, sugar, and rolled oats in a bowl.
2. Stir in the cocoa powder and then the cold coffee.
3. Stir in the liquor or cognac.
4. Shape into balls and roll in chocolate sprinkles. Store in the refrigerator.

## lion bars

MAKES 20 BARS

1 3/4 cups crunchy peanut butter
3/4 cup plus 2 tablespoons golden syrup or light corn syrup
1/2 cup sugar
1 tablespoon vanilla sugar
1 2/3 cups unsweetened coconut
2 1/2 cups Rice Krispies
9 oz good-quality dark chocolate (70% cocoa solids)

1. Melt the peanut butter, syrup, sugar, and vanilla sugar over a low heat.
2. Toast the unsweetened coconut in a dry frying pan.
3. Stir in the coconut and Rice Krispies into the mixture.
4. Divide the mixture into two rectangular loaf pans lined with plastic wrap.
5. Leave to set in the refrigerator for about 1 1/2 hours.
6. Melt the chocolate in a bowl set over a pan of simmering water. Cut the cake into three-fourth in bars and dip into the melted chocolate.
7. Put back into the refrigerator and leave to set for a few hours.

## chocolate radio cake

The heyday of the radio cake was in the 1930s and 1940s when the radio was in fashion. The story goes that the cake got its name because it resembles the loudspeaker of an old-fashioned radio.

MAKES 1 CAKE

3/4 cup plus 2 tablespoons heavy whipping cream
1/2 cup milk
3 tablespoons honey
11 oz good quality dark chocolate (70% cocoa solids)
1 tablespoon unsalted butter
4 oz lady fingers or vanilla wafers

1. Bring the cream, milk, and honey to the boil.
2. Remove the saucepan from the heat and add the finely chopped chocolate. Stir until the chocolate melts. Add the butter bit by bit.
3. Line a loaf pan with plastic wrap. Pour in a thin layer of the mixture. Add a layer of biscuits.
4. Continue layering the mixture and biscuits, ending with mixture. Leave in the refrigerator overnight.
5. Turn the cake out of the pan and cut into slices while it's still cold.

## chocolate coconut bomb

MAKES 15

1/2 cup unsalted butter, softened
1/2 cup plus 2 tablespoons sugar
1 1/4 cups rolled oats
1 teaspoon vanilla sugar
1/4 cup good-quality cocoa powder
3 tablespoons cold coffee
unsweetened coconut

1. Mix together the butter, sugar, and the rolled oats in a bowl.
2. Stir in the vanilla sugar and the cocoa powder. Add the coffee.
3. Shape into balls and roll in unsweetened coconut. Store in the refrigerator.

## mint crisp

MAKES 15 PIECES

11 oz good-quality dark chocolate (70% cocoa solids)
a few drops peppermint flavoring
3/4 cup bran flakes
4 oz homemade almond paste, see recipe page 208

1. Melt one-third of the chocolate in a bowl set over a pan of simmering water. Chop the remaining chocolate finely.
2. Remove the melted chocolate from the heat and stir in the chopped chocolate. Add a few drops of peppermint flavoring.
3. Leave the chocolate to cool completely. Stir occasionally until it starts to thicken and you can see marks from the spoon.
4. Blend in the bran flakes and grated almond paste. Stir just enough to cover the bran flakes evenly.
5. Drop the mixture in small peaks onto a sheet of parchment paper and leave to set in the refrigerator.

## rocky road

These really are the best sweets in the world.

MAKES 20 PIECES

5 oz good-quality dark chocolate (70% cocoa solids)
2 bags toffees
2 handfuls of mini marshmallows
1 1/3 cups salted peanuts
3/4 cup peeled pistachios

1. Melt the chocolate in a bowl set over a pan of simmering water. Leave to cool a little.
2. Chop the toffees and mix all the ingredients with the melted chocolate.
3. Pour the mixture into a square baking tin lined with parchment paper to a depth of 1 in. Leave to set in the refrigerator, then cut into squares.

## chocolate truffles

This basic truffle recipe can be varied with all kinds of delicious flavorings. You can use chili and ground cinnamon, lemon zest, peppermint flavoring, dark rum, whisky, ground ginger, or crushed cardamom. Alternatively, roll the truffles in different kinds of flavored sugar. I use demerara sugar mixed with crushed cardamom or ground cinnamon. It's also really nice to mix sugar with lemon or orange zest (but let the mix dry first).

MAKES 20

9 oz good-quality dark chocolate (70% cocoa solids)
1/2 cup heavy whipping cream
3 tablespoons honey
1 tablespoon unsalted butter
1 pinch flaked salt
cocoa powder

1. Finely chop the the chocolate.
2. Bring the heavy whipping cream and honey to the boil and pour the mixture over the chocolate stirring continually. Add the butter and the flaked salt and mix thoroughly.
3. Pour the chocolate into a plastic food container with a lid and leave to set in the refrigerator for about 4 hours.
4. Shape the chocolate into balls (truffles) and roll them in cocoa powder.

## chocolate chip granola bar

MAKES 20

1 1/2 cups dried figs
1 tablespoon good quality cocoa powder
1 tablespoon warm espresso coffee
1 1/3 cups golden raisins
2 1/4 cups granola with dried fruits
1/2 cup cornflakes
7 oz good quality dark chocolate (70% cocoa solids)

1. Cut the stems off the figs and chop them coarsely.
2. Mix them in a blender together with the cocoa powder and coffee.
3. Add half of the raisins and the granola. Process for a few seconds to make a paste.
4. Transfer the paste to a bowl and pour in the remaining raisins, granola, and cornflakes.
5. Chop the chocolate and mix half of it into the paste.
6. Roll out the paste between two sheets of parchment paper until it is one-half in thick.
7. Melt the remaining chocolate in a bowl set over a pan of simmering water. Brush the cake with the chocolate.
8. Leave to set in the refrigerator. Cut the cake into pieces when the chocolate has set.

# sauces, creams & marmalades

It's what's on the inside that counts. Many of our cakes would not reach their true glory without their beautiful and tasty fillings. Vanilla cream, elderflower cream, and lemon curd are a few of the key performers on my baking stage. In this chapter you will find some of my favorite marmalade and jam recipes together with other indispensible accessories for buns, pies, and desserts. Pick and choose your favorites from these lovely recipes.

## speedy vanilla custard

SERVES 4

½ vanilla pod
3 organic egg yolks
3 ½ tablespoons sugar
1 cup heavy whipping cream

1. Split the vanilla pod lengthways and scrape out the seeds.
2. Beat together the egg yolks, sugar, and vanilla seeds until pale and creamy.
3. Whip the cream until it is softly peaking and blend it into the egg mixture.


## exotic mango sauce

SERVES 4

1 large ripe mango
¼ cup plus 3 tablespoons sugar
½ cup water
1 tablespoon light rum
zest and juice of 1 lime

1. Peel the mango, remove the pit, and cut the flesh into pieces.
2. Boil the mango with the sugar and water for about 5 minutes.
3. Flavor with the rum and lime zest and juice.
4. Use a hand-held mixer to blend the sauce until smooth.
5. Strain the sauce through a fine sieve and leave to cool.


## homemade almond paste

MAKES 1 ¼ LB (OR 17 ½ OZ)

1 ½ cups almonds
1 cup sugar

1. Blanch the almonds.
2. Process the almonds in a blender to a fine powder.
3. Add the sugar and mix for 5–7 minutes to make a smooth paste.


## forest berry sauce

SERVES 4

¾ cup fresh or frozen strawberries or blueberries
½ cup sugar
½ cup water
juice of 1 lemon

1. In a stainless steel saucepan bring the berries, sugar, water, and lemon juice to a boil and simmer for about 5 minutes.
2. Mix until smooth using a hand blender.
3. Strain the sauce through a fine sieve. Leave to cool.


## crème patisserie

The most difficult part of making crème patisserie is simmering to thicken. It is important to beat the mixture continually during this process. As soon as the custard has thickened you have to pour it into a cold bowl. Never put your fingers in it because it separates easily.

MAKES ENOUGH FOR 1 CAKE

1 vanilla pod
2 cups plus 2 tablespoons milk
½ cup plus 2 tablespoons sugar
7 organic egg yolks
⅔ cup cornstarch
¼ cup unsalted butter, softened

1. Halve the vanilla pod lengthways and scrape out the seeds. Bring the milk and vanilla seeds to a boil in a saucepan. Strain out the vanilla seeds.
2. Beat together the eggs, sugar, and cornstarch until pale and fluffy in a bowl.
3. Pour the hot milk into the egg mixture, beating continuously.
4. Pour the mixture back into the saucepan and heat, beating all the time. Pour into a cold bowl when it has thickened substantially.
5. Melt the butter and add it to the custard, beating until it is completely incorporated.
6. Transfer to the refrigerator.

## lime curd

MAKES 1 SMALL JAR

6 limes

1/2 cup plus 2 tablespoons sugar

1/4 cup butter

3 tablespoons cornstarch

2 organic eggs

2 organic egg yolks

1. Mix the zest and juice of four limes.
2. Bring the lime juice, zest, sugar, and butter to a boil.
3. Strain the liquid.
4. Blend the cornstarch with the juice from remaining limes. Stir into the warm liquid.
5. Beat the eggs and stir into the liquid. Return the saucepan to the heat and simmer, stirring constantly, until the curd thickens.
6. Pour into a clean jar or bowl and leave to cool.

## lemon curd

MAKES 1 SMALL JAR

3 lemons

1/2 cup plus 2 tablepoons sugar

1/4 cup unsalted butter

3 tablespoons cornstarch

2 organic eggs

2 organic egg yolks

1. Mix the zest of three lemons with juice of two lemons and bring to a boil with the sugar and butter.
2. Strain the liquid.
3. Blend the cornstarch with the juice from the remaining lemon. Stir into the warm liquid.
4. Beat the eggs and yolks and stir into the liquid, put the saucepan back on the heat and simmer, stirring constantly, until the curd thickens.
5. Pour into a clean jar or bowl and leave to cool.

## raspberry sauce with vanilla

SERVES 4

1/2 cup sugar

1/2 cup water

1/2 vanilla pod

1 1/3 cups fresh or frozen raspberries

juice of 1 lime

3 tablespoons crème de cassis (optional)

1. In a stainless steel saucepan bring the sugar, water, and the vanilla pod to a boil.
2. Add the raspberries and boil for about 5 minutes.
3. Add the lime juice and the crème de cassis.
4. Remove the vanilla pod and mix the sauce until smooth with a hand-held blender.
5. Strain the sauce through a fine sieve. Leave to cool.

## granny-style vanilla sauce

SERVES 4

1 cup milk

1/2 vanilla pod

3 1/2 tablespoons sugar

4 organic egg yolks

1/4 cup cornstarch

2 tablespoons unsalted butter, softened

1/2 cup heavy whipping cream

1. Halve the vanilla pod and scrape out the seeds. Bring the milk, vanilla pod, and seeds to a boil in a saucepan. Remove the vanilla pod after the milk has boiled.
2. Beat the sugar, the egg yolk, and the cornstarch until white and fluffy.
3. Pour the hot milk into the egg mixture beating continuously.
4. Pour the mixture back into the saucepan and heat beating continuously. When the custard has thickened substantially, pour into a cold bowl.
5. Add the butter and beat into the warm custard.
6. Chill the custard in the refrigerator.
7. Whip the cream lightly and blend into the cream to make a fluffy vanilla sauce.

## zabaglione

Zabaglione is a dessert made of egg yolks, sugar, and sweet liquor (usually Marsala), and sometimes cream and whole eggs. The zabaglione is a very light and airy custard, which is beaten to incorporate a lot of air. Zabaglione is traditionally served together with fresh dates. This custard is perfect together with any fresh berries or as a sauce to go with apple pie or crumble.

SERVES 4

4 organic egg yolks
1/2 cup sugar
1/2 cup Marsala

1. Put all the ingredients in a stainless steel bowl over a pan of simmering water.
2. Beat until fluffy. You should see distinct marks from the whisk in the cream.
3. Remove the bowl from the pan carefully and continue to beat for about 1 minute until the cream has cooled a bit.

## elderflower custard

This custard is a wonderful cake filling. It is also perfect as an accompaniment for cakes and pies, but you should use half the quantity of cornstarch because you don't want the custard as thick.

MAKES ENOUGH FOR 1 CAKE

4 organic egg yolks
3 1/2 tablespoons sugar
3 tablespoons cornstarch
1/4 cup undiluted elderflower juice
1 cup heavy whipping cream

1. Beat the egg yolks and the sugar until pale and fluffy.
2. Mix the cornstarch with the elderflower juice.
3. Bring the cream to a boil and blend with the juice. Mix the warm liquid into the egg mixture.
4. Pour the custard back into the saucepan and simmer, beating until the custard has thickened. Leave to cool.

## syrup

MAKES 1 SMALL BOTTLE

3/4 cup sugar
1/2 cup water
juice of 1 lemon

1. Bring all the ingredients to a boil,
2. Leave to cool and pour into a bottle or a bowl. Seal carefully.

## classic chocolate sauce

The vegetable oil makes the finished sauce glossy. Always use good quality cocoa powder for sauces, desserts, and cakes.

SERVES 4

1/2 cup good-quality cocoa powder
3/4 cup sugar
1/2 cup water
1 tablespoon vegetable oil

1. Mix together the cocoa powder, sugar, and water. Boil for about 3 minutes.
2. Add the oil and either serve the sauce warm or leave to cool.

## chocolate fudge sauce

SERVES 4

1/2 cup milk
1/2 cup heavy whipping cream
3 tablespoons brown sugar
1/4 cup golden syrup or light corn syrup
1 teaspoon ground ginger
4 oz milk chocolate
4 oz good quality chocolate (70% cocoa solids)
1 tablespoon unsalted butter

1. Bring the milk, heavy whipping cream, brown sugar, syrup, and ginger to a boil. Leave to cool.
2. Chop the chocolate finely, then stir into the sauce together with the butter.

## butterscotch sauce

Chill a plate in the freezer. Spoon a little sauce onto the plate to check the consistency. The longer you boil it, the thicker the sauce will be. Add lime zest or ground cardamom to give this classic sauce a modern twist.

SERVES 4

1 cup heavy whipping cream
3 ½ tablespoons sugar
½ cup golden syrup or light corn syrup
1 teaspoon good quality cocoa powder

1. Let the ingredients boil for about 20 minutes in a heavy-bottomed saucepan. Leave to cool.

## vanilla crème fraîche

When you buy vanilla pods you should look for soft, dark, and juicy ones. The vanilla pods lose their aroma when they turn dry and hard. Store the pods in a dark, cool, and airtight place to keep them fresh.

SERVES 4

1 cup crème fraîche
½ vanilla pod
3 tablespoons confectioner's sugar

1. Whip the crème fraîche with an electric mixer until it is softly peaking.
2. Split a vanilla pod lengthways and scrape out the seeds. Mix the seeds with the crème fraîche.
3. Add confectioner's sugar.

## fromage blanc

SERVES 4

½ cup heavy whipping cream
1 cup low-fat Greek yogurt
3 tablespoons confectioner's sugar

1. Whip the cream until it is softly peaking.
2. Mix with the yogurt and add the confectioner's sugar.

## butterscotch cream

An easy shortcut is to buy ready-made fudge if you don't want to make your own.

SERVES 4

1 cup heavy whipping cream
5 tablespoons cold butterscotch sauce

1. Whip the cream until fluffy and mix with the fudge sauce.

## raspberry fool cream

SERVES 4

1 cup heavy whipping cream
½ cup low-fat Greek yogurt
¼ cup raspberries
3 tablespoons confectioner's sugar

1. Whip the cream until softly peaking and mix with the yogurt.
2. Mash the raspberries lightly with the confectioner's sugar.
3. Flavor the cream with the raspberries.

## chocolate & raspberry marmalade

Sterilize jars before filling with jam or marmalade. Wash them thoroughly. Put them in the oven upside down on a wire rack at 250°F for about 30 minutes or plunge them into boiling water.

MAKES 1 JAR

1 ¾ cups frozen raspberries
1 ¾ cups muscovado sugar
3 oz cup good-quality dark chocolate
   (70% cocoa solids)

1. Simmer the raspberries and the sugar in a saucepan for about 15 minutes. Skim if needed.
2. Take the saucepan off the heat and melt coarsely chopped chocolate into the mixture.
3. Leave the marmalade to cool a bit before pouring into a sterilized glass jar and close the lid tightly.

sauces, creams & marmalades

## rhubarb & ginger marmalade

Chill a small plate in the freezer. Spoon a little of the warm marmalade onto the chilled plate and push the marmalade with a spoon. It's ready if it won't run back straightaway.

MAKES 2 JARS
4 large rhubarb sticks
1 ½ in fresh root ginger
½ vanilla pod
juice of 1 lemon
¼ cup water
9 ½ cups preserving sugar
a few drops of red food coloring

1. Rinse and chop the rhubarb into small pieces, discarding any stringy bits. Slice the ginger thinly. Split the vanilla pod lengthways and scrape out the seeds.
2. Mix all the ingredients except the sugar in a heavy-bottomed saucepan and allow to boil uncovered for about 15 minutes.
3. Stir in the sugar, boil for a few minutes uncovered, skimming if needed.
4. Remove the vanilla pod out and leave the marmalade to cool a bit. Color the marmalade with a few drops of food coloring. Pour the marmalade into warm, sterilized jars and close the lids tightly.

## strawberry jam

MAKES 2 JARS
4 ½ cups fresh strawberries
1 vanilla pod
1 tablespoon water
2 ¾ cups sugar
1 ¼ cups preserving sugar
zest and juice of 1 lime

1. Hull and halve the strawberries.
2. Split the vanilla pod lengthways and scrape out the seeds. Boil the strawberries for about 15 minutes together with the water and the vanilla seeds. Skim if needed.
3. Add the sugar, preserving sugar, lime zest, and

lime juice and bring to a boil.
4. Leave the jam to cool a bit before pouring it into warm, sterilized glass jars.

## tomato & lemongrass marmalade

MAKES 2 JARS
2 ¼ lb (about 6 ¼ cups) organic tomatoes
3 stalks of lemongrass
zest and juice of 1 lemon
9 ½ cups preserving sugar

1. Rinse and dice the tomatoes and put them in a saucepan.
2. Crush the lemongrass with the back of a knife to release the flavor.
3. Put the lemongrass in the saucepan together with the lemon zest and juice and boil, covered, for about 15 minutes.
4. Stir in the preserving sugar, boil uncovered for a few minutes. Skim if needed.
5. Take out the lemongrass and leave the marmalade to cool a bit. Pour into warm, sterilized glass jars.

## blackcurrant jam

MAKES ABOUT 1 LB
3 ½ lb (about 20 cups) blackcurrants
1 vanilla pod
1 tablespoon water
2 ¾ cups sugar
1 ¼ cups preserving sugar
zest and juice of 1 lemon

1. Rinse and pick the berries. Split the vanilla pod lengthways and scrape out the seeds. Put the berries in a saucepan with the water and vanilla seeds.
2. Boil uncovered for about 15 minutes and skim if needed.
3. Add the sugar, preserving sugar, lemon zest, and lemon juice. Bring to a boil.
4. Leave the jam to cool a bit before pouring it into warm, sterilized glass jars.

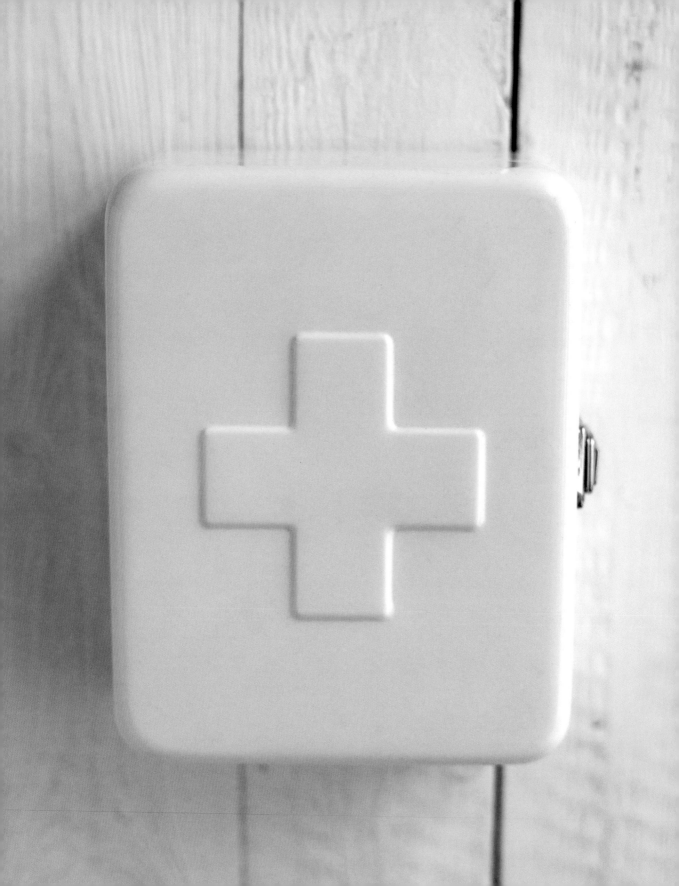

# sos in the kitchen

**Why is the dough not rising?**
- The liquid used in making the dough may have been too warm. If the liquid's temperature is over 100°F, there is a risk that the yeast will be killed, which will stop the dough from rising.
- The dough liquid may have been too cold, which is not actually wrong but will mean that the dough will take longer to rise. The advantage is that this gives the flavors longer to develop, so your bread will be tastier!
- The yeast may be too old. Don't forget to check the expiration date on the packet.
- The flour may have been too cold, which means the dough will take longer to rise. It is better to use flour at room temperature.
- The dough may be standing somewhere too cold or in a draft. Doughs like to be in a warm, even temperature where they can prove evenly. You can actually use this to control how fast the dough rises. Put the dough in a slightly cooler place if you want it to take its time, or a warmer place if you want to work faster.
- There may be too much flour in the dough, which makes it heavier and reduces its capacity to rise.

**Why is the dough heavy instead of soft and elastic?**
- If there is too much flour in the dough, it will become heavy and dense.
- The dough may have been kneaded for too long after the first rising. It often needs no more than one fold or two, depending on what type of bread you are baking.
- There may be insufficient salt. This makes it lifeless, reduces its capacity to prove and leaves it less springy.

- There may be too much fat or sugar in the dough. It will prove but will take longer than usual.

**Why is the bread heavy instead of light and fluffy?**
- The dough may not have been given long enough to rise. My rule of thumb is to let it double in size.
- The oven may have been too cold or the bread may not have been in for long enough, which will give a heavier bread. If the bread does have enough color but still needs to be baked for longer, cover it with some aluminum foil so it can stay in a bit longer without burning.

**Why are the cookies and bars so hard?**
- There may not have been enough yeast or baking powder in the dough.
- There might have been too much sugar or too little butter in the dough.
- The bars may have been cut up before they were cool enough. This can cause the edges to harden when they finally cool.

**Why are the rolls dry or hard?**
- There may have been too much flour in the dough, which will make them dry.
- There may have been too little fat in the dough, which will also make them dry.
- The buns may not have been given long enough to prove on the tray, which could make them hard.
- The buns may have been in the oven for too long. Try raising the temperature and shortening the baking time.

Why is the cake bulging over the edge of the tin?
- The tin may be too small or was too full. It should be no more than two-thirds full when you put it in the oven.

What made the sponge, muffins, or scones chewy or rubbery?
- Never whisk flour into a mixture containing baking powder. This draws out the gluten, making the bread tough and dense.
- The flour may have been mixed into the batter for too long. Blend it in just enough to mix it evenly and no more.

What caused the cake to crack?
- The baking powder or baking soda may not have been mixed evenly into the batter. Always mix baking powder or baking soda into the dry ingredients before blending them into the mixture.
- There may have been too much flour added to the mixture.
- The oven may have been a bit too hot. Try a lower temperature next time.

Why has the cake stuck to the tin?
- The tin may not have been greased well enough. Try cooling the tin down with a damp tea towel. This should make it easier to loosen the cake from the tin.
- Let the cake cool down before trying to remove it from the tin.
- I generally use nonstick pans. I am careful to make sure that I always keep older tins greased with some cooking oil when they are not in use.

Why is the cake not rising?
- There may not be enough baking powder mixed in.
- The oven door may have been opened too often. Cakes need an even temperature to rise.
- The mixture may not have been whisked for long enough before the flour was added. Egg and sugar should be whisked up until fluffy and

pale. Butter and sugar should be whisked until light and creamy.
- The mixture may have been stirred for too long after the flour and baking powder or baking soda was added. This will reduce the cake's ability to rise.

Why did the fruit or berries sink to the bottom of the cake?
- The dough may have been too light to support the filling. Try rolling the fruit pieces or berries in a little flour before you add them to the mixture.
- Add a little more flour to the mixture next time.

Why is the cookie dough crumbly?
- There may be too little liquid in the dough. Add a drop of water and the dough should bind together better.
- Some cookie doughs are supposed to be very dry, such as the dream cookies. You just need to squeeze the dough into small balls, which then flatten out on the baking tray.

Why is the cookie dough so hard to roll out?
- Some doughs are tougher than others to roll out so it can be a good idea to roll a bit, have a break so the dough can rest and then have another go.
- There may be too much flour in the dough, making it dense and firm. Sprinkle some water on to the countertop, which gives the dough a better grip and makes it easier to roll out.
- There might be too little flour in the dough. Add a little extra flour and roll out on a well floured surface.

Why are the dream cookies so dense?
- The oven temperature may not have been quite right or the cookies may have been in for too long. If the oven is too warm, the cookies will get more color. Ideally, they should stay pale and not be colored at all.
- Smaller dream cookies need less time in the over; larger ones take longer.

Why are the cookies becoming too flat on the baking sheet?

- Some cookies should flatten and others not. Check the recipe and take a look at the picture to see how they should look.
- There may have been too much flour in the dough. If you have any dough left over, work a little more flour into the dough and try baking a couple of cookies as a test.
- The oven may have been too hot. Try reducing the temperature next time.

Why is the cake or bread browning on the outside but is still not done on the inside?

- The baking tin may have been too high in the oven. Cover the cake or bread with some aluminum foil so it can stay in longer without burning.
- The cake or bread may have been in at too high a temperature for too short a time.
- The oven may have been too hot. Try reducing the temperature next time so the cake or bread can be in a little longer.
- If the bottom starts to burn, you can put an extra baking tray near the bottom of the oven to absorb some of the heat.

What is the difference between a conventional oven and a fan oven?

- A fan oven is more efficient and spreads the heat more evenly in the oven, which makes it ideal for baking. Bread is baked more evenly and rises better. A fan oven has a more powerful heating effect, which means that oven times may need to be reduced in some cases. I always bake my bread and cakes in a fan oven, so my recipes assume you are using one too. If you are using a conventional oven, you may need to increase the baking times slightly. Consult the manufacturer's handbook.

Why did the jam, juice, or marmalade go mouldy or bubbly?

- You should never dip your finger into the boiled marmalade or jam because it will quickly go bad if it comes into contact with saliva or bacteria.
- The berries you used may have been dirty or past their best. Take care to clean and rinse berries that are to be used for jam or squash.
- All the froth may not have been scooped off during boiling. The froth contains natural bacteria and fungi, which should be removed by scooping off the froth while boiling.
- The bottles or jars may not have been sterilised. Stand the empty bottles or jars upside down in an oven at 250°F or dip them into boiling water to sterilise them. Don't forget to sterilise the tops and caps too.
- The storage area may have been too warm. Jam and marmalade should be stored in a cool, dark place. Open containers need to be stored in a refrigerator.
- The jars or bottles may not have been closed tightly enough. Double check the lids.
- The boiling time may have been too short. Both jam and marmalade should be boiled for quite a while.

Why is the jam or marmalade so runny?

- If you used regular, granulated sugar there may not have been enough pectin in the fruit or the berries. You can mix regular sugar and preserving sugar together, fifty-fifty, for a thicker consistency.
- Some fruits and berries are high in pectin and so they jell more easily. Most fruits and berries need added pectin, however. Pectin can be added in a pure form or you can use special preserving sugar, which is pre-mixed with pectin.
- If the jam or marmalade is still too runny after a few days, bring to the boil again and use more pectin.
- The jam or marmalade may not have been boiled for long enough. If you boil for a little longer, the liquid will be reduced and the jam or marmalade will set more firmly.

# kitchen magic

Yeast consists of living fungi which must be handled carefully if they are to do their job. The yeast transforms sugar into carbon dioxide through chemical and biological processes. This causes the dough to expand and rise, making it porous. You can use either fresh or dry yeast.

I always like to cook with fresh yeast, but because it is not readily available in many places, dry yeast has been substituted in these recipes. Fresh yeast must be stored in the fridge and used before the expiration date on the packet. If you decide to use fresh yeast, bear in mind that the liquid used in making the dough must not be over 100°F or the yeast will die. The dough should be allowed to stand at room temperature in an even, draft-free space while it is rising.

Dried yeast is made from fresh yeast that has been dried and granulated. It is sold in ¼ oz sachets and does not need to be refrigerated.

Easy-blend or fast-action yeast, which is widely available, is also available in ¼ oz sachets. Use one sachet of easy-blend or fast-action yeast for every 3 ¼ lb of all-purpose flour. In general, you will need about twice as much fresh yeast as dried or easy-blend yeast, but this will vary according to the type of flour and the other ingredients. To avoid a strong, yeasty flavor, err on the side of caution and use less, rather than more, yeast and leave the dough to prove for longer.

Sourdough is made from water and flour, which gives the dough more flavor and more capacity to rise. It also gives a slightly chewier result. Many bread connoisseurs consider sourdough a must. It contains natural yeast and bacteria, which give a sour, fresh taste.

You can sometimes buy a cup of sourdough from a proper bakery. Keep it refrigerated in a jar, but take it out of the fridge the day before baking, or at least a few hours ahead. Dilute with water and flour until it goes thick, like waffle batter. After a while, it will come to life and start bubbling.

Baking soda is a naturally occurring substance that produces good, light cakes. It needs to be mixed with something acidic—like syrup or jam—to kick-off the expansion process. Then it works like yeast where carbon dioxide forms inside the dough or cake mixture, making it light and airy.

You can swap baking soda for baking powder in the ratio of 1 teaspoon baking soda to 2 teaspoons baking powder.

Baking powder is mix of baking soda, acid salts, and starch which is ideal for baking soft cakes and muffins. The expansion process begins before the cake is put in the oven. Store in an airtight container, otherwise it will not function properly.

# BAKE
## A WISH

# recipe index

# tastes

tastes

223

# A warm thank you to . . .

Everyone who has contributed to this special baking book.

The Muffin Mafia, my mum and my grandmothers, but above all to my little sister Petronella for her helping hand with the baking, tasting and photographing.

Ulrika and Sten-Åke Magnusson for all your support and for letting me stay at your beautiful bed and breakfast "In my garden" in Mariefred. An extra special thank you to you, Ulrika, for helping out with the stage design at the photo-shoots.

Sweet little Ebba for tasting the high-hat cupcakes.

Photographer Wolfgang Kleinschmidt for all the beautiful pictures in the book and for your enthusiasm and creativity. www.kleinschmidt.se

Mikael Engblom for the perfect graphic design, which has led to another wonderful book. Mats Carlson for production management.

Tomas Ringqvist for the beautiful pictures on pages 8, 39, 73, 141, 142 and 198.

Skyhorse Publishing books may be purchased in bulk at special discounts for sales promotion, corporate gifts, fund-raising, or educational purposes. Special editions can also be created to specifications. For details, contact the Special Sales Department, Skyhorse Publishing, 555 Eighth Avenue, Suite 903, New York, NY 10018 or info@skyhorsepublishing.com.

www.skyhorsepublishing.com

10 9 8 7 6 5 4 3 2 1

Library of Congress Cataloging-in-Publication Data

Lindholm, Leila.
  Sweet and savory Swedish baking / Leila Lindholm.
    p. cm.
  ISBN 978-1-60239-798-9 (alk. paper)
  1. Baking--Sweden. 2. Cookery, Swedish.
I. Title.
  TX763.L56 2009
  641.59485--dc22

                          2009013205

Printed in Singapore